고급 번역과 영작 연습

Practice in Translating Korean into English and
Writing in English at an Advanced Level

고급 번역과 영작 연습

© 이응호, 2017

1판 1쇄 인쇄__2017년 02월 20일
1판 1쇄 발행__2017년 02월 25일

지은이__이응호
펴낸이__홍정표

펴낸곳__글로벌콘텐츠
　　　　등록__제 25100-2008-24호

공급처__(주)글로벌콘텐츠출판그룹
　　　　대표__홍정표　이사__양정섭　편집디자인__김미미　기획·마케팅__노경민 이종훈
　　　　주소__서울특별시 강동구 천중로 196 정일빌딩 401호　전화__02-488-3280　팩스__02-488-3281
　　　　홈페이지__www.gcbook.co.kr

값 15,000원
ISBN 979-11-5852-132-5 03740

고급
번역과
영작
연습

Practice in Translating Korean into English and
Writing in English at an Advanced Level

이응호 지음

"영어 공부에는 왕도가 없다"는 말이 있다. 한 두 달이면 자막 없이 영어를 본다는 식의 터무니 없는 상술이 난무하는 요즘에 이 말의 진리는 더욱 빛을 발한다. 번역도 마찬가지다. 좋은 영어 글에 많이 노출되어 한국어와 영어 간의 구문, 표현법 등에 대한 통찰력을 키우고, 문법 규칙, 단어나 관용어 등의 의미 및 활용 문맥을 정확히 익혀서 번역을 많이 해보는 것 외에는 왕도가 없다.

미국에서의 오랜 유학과 생활 경험 및 한국외대통번역대학원에서 번역과목을 직접 지도하셨던 교육 경험을 바탕으로 이응호 교수님이 저술하신 본 번역학습서는 그와 같은 정통파식 학습법을 지향한다는 데서 반갑기 그지 없다.

원문의 의미를 다양한 방식으로 표현할 수 있는 능력은 훌륭한 번역사의 핵심 역량이다. 본 학습서는 다양한 주제의 신문 사설을 사용한 실제 한영 번역 연습을 통해서 그와 같은 역량을 갖춘 번역사의 길로 독자를 인도한다.

번역은 전문 번역사만 하는 것이 아니다. 일반 영어학습자들도 자신의 생각을 말이나 글로 표현하기 전에 머리 속에서 번역을 하는 경우가 많다. 이와 같은 머릿속 번역에서도 우리말 표현이나 구조를 그대로 영어로 옮기려 하면 문제가 발생한다. 따라서 우리말에 대응하는 다양한 영어식 표현을 익히는 것은 영어다운 말과 글을 쓰는데도 필수적이다.

이같은 면에서 번역을 공부하는 학생뿐만 아니라 세련된 영어 글을 쓰는 법을 익히고 싶은 영어 학습자들에게 필독을 권한다.

이창수

(한국외국어대학교 통역번역대학원 교수, 국제회의통역사, 문학번역가)

영어 글쓰기 능력을 키우기 위해서는 여러 가지 방법이 있지만 이 책에서는 한·영 번역을 통해 그에 필요한 영어 어휘와 문장구조를 숙달하는 데 역점을 두었다. 한·영 번역은 대체로 두 가지 과정을 거쳐야 한다. 첫째로, 한글 원문의 내용을 정확히 파악하고 그 내용이 어떤 문체로 표현되는지를 결정해야 한다. 다음은 원문의 내용과 그것이 전달된 문체를 그에 해당하는 영어 표현으로 정확하게 대치시키는 작업이다.

흔히 영어 번역은 완벽할 수 없다고들 한다. (There's always something missing in translation.) 원문의 내용과 표현이 번역문에 그대로 자연스럽게 반영되지 못하기 때문인데, 이와 같은 결함은 각 언어 사용자들의 서로 다른 문화와 생활 양식에서 오는 불가피한 결과일 것이다. 그러나 엄밀히 말해서 번역(translation/ controlled writing) 뿐만 아니라 영어내 표현에 있어서도 완전한 동의어나 동의문은 존재하지 않는다. 그 이유는 두 개의 동의어가 서로 유사한 의미를 공유하지만 동시에 다른 의미 양상을 띄고 있어 서로가 바꿔 쓰일 수 없기 때문이다. 그래서 때로는 번역문이 원문에 비해 더 길거나 짧게 표현되는 경우가 허다하다.

따라서 한글을 영어로 옮길 때 유의해야 할 점은 영어의 다양한 문체, 예컨대 격식(formal), 비격식(informal) 또는 회화체(colloquial)를 나타내는 단어나 문장 구조를 올바르게 선정하는 것이다. 특히 영어 단어는 기본적인 의

미 이외에도 의미상의 범위, 동작의 지속성, 함축, 비유 등 여러 특성과 함께 다양한 문장 구조를 이끄는 개념이 포함되어 어떤 단어를 사용하느냐에 따라 각기 다른 형태의 문형과 문체가 생성된다. 또한 원문의 의미상 불필요한 표현은 생략(deletion)하고 원문에서는 생략된 표현을 첨가(addition)시키며, 필요하면 원문의 문장 구조를 영어식 구문으로 변형(transformation)시켜야 하는 경우가 많다.

뿐만 아니라 한국어 사용자는 습관상 동사를 수식하는 부사를 덧붙여 사용하는 경우가 많은데 영어는 동사 내에 부사의 뜻이 포함되어 영어 표현을 그만큼 축소시킬 수 있다. 이처럼 다양한 의미 양상을 띤 영어 단어는 영어 전달 과정에서 언어사용자 양자간의 인식(perception)에도 적지 않은 영향을 미친다. 예를 들면 영어를 외국어로 배우는 학습자와 원어민의 대화에서 의사소통이 원만하게 이루어지지 못하는 경우가 많은데 이는 일반적으로 영어학습자들이 원어민들도 좀처럼 사용하지 않는 지나친 격식체와 전문적인 영어 표현을 선호하는 경향이 있기 때문이다.

이처럼 복잡한 영어 단어와 구문 형태를 활용하기 위해서는 한·영 번역 시 새로운 낱말이나 문장을 다룰 때 기본적인 의미를 포착하는 데만 만족할 것이 아니라 그와 같은 표현이 언제 어디서 어떻게, 또는 어떤 상황에서 어떤 단어와 함께 사용할 수 있는지를 확인하면서 배우는 학습 태도가 필요하다.

이와 함께 영어의 격식체를 비격식체와 회화체 그리고 문맥에 따라서 속어 (slang)로 바꾸거나, 또는 반대로 변형시키는 연습을 하면 다양한 영어문체를 구사할 수 있는 능력을 키우는데 큰 도움이 된다.

　이러한 점을 염두에 두고 필자는 국내 일간 신문, 잡지에 실린 기사 중에서 일부를 발췌하여(권미 출전 목록 참조) 현대식 영어 표현으로 번역한 후 설명을 상세히 실었다. 물론 이 밖에도 여러 가지 다른 형태의 번역이 가능하지만 그것은 독자의 과제로 남기고 싶다. 끝으로 이 책이 완성되기까지 세밀한 교정과 정정을 하는데 시간과 노력을 아끼지 않은 홍현주 박사에게 참으로 고맙다는 말을 전한다.

이 응 호

Part 3 사회

Part 4 교육

Part 5 건강

Part 6 결혼

Part 7 기후

고급
번역과
영작
연습

Practice in Translating Korean into English and
Writing in English at an Advanced Level

Part 1

정치

1

정치인의 관심

번역과 영작

정치인에 대한 신뢰와 지지가 바로 그 정치인의 영향력으로 환산되고 그 영
향력으로 정치인은 정치를 하게 된다. 여기서 문제는 복잡하고 바쁜 현대사회
에서 국민 한 사람 한 사람이 그 정치인을 수시로 만나서 어떤 사람인지 직접
객관적으로 확인할 방법이 없다는 데 있다. 결국 국민들은 그 정치인이 "어떻
게 보이느냐"에 좌우되어 그를 지지하고 신뢰하고 표를 던지는 것이 현실이고,
따라서 정치인은 "남들에게 어떻게 보이느냐"에 가장 신경을 쓸 수밖에 없다.

(한국일보 2012.03.29.)

* * *

Public confidence in the politicians and their approval ratings
normally turn into their political clout, which they then use to engage
in their political activities.

The problem, however, is that the complex and hectic life in modern society makes it hardly possible for the people to find ways to meet one-on-one with the politicians whenever they want so they can size them up in a more direct and objective way.

The reality, therefore, is that the decision made by the people to support, trust and vote for any particular politicians is often influenced by how they are perceived by the general public.

As a result, the politicians are left with no choice but to concern themselves with the way they appear to other people.

 해설

1. 정치인에 대한 신뢰와 지지가 바로 그 정치인의 영향력으로 환산되고 그 영향력으로 정치인은 정치를 하게 된다.

>>> Public confidence in the politicians and their approval ratings normally turn into their political clout, which they then use to engage in their political activities.

• **public confidence in the politician:** 정치인에 대한 일반 대중의 신뢰

• **confidence in:** ~에 대한 신뢰 **cf have/ put confidence in:** ~을 신뢰하다

• **the politicians' approval ratings:** 정치가에 대한 지지율 (= the number of the people who agreed with their policies)

- **turn into:** ~으로 바뀌다 (= be transformed into)

  He (was) turned into a politician. 그는 정치가로 변신했다.

- **political clout:** 정치적 영향력 (= political power/ influence/ weight)

- **use clout:** 영향력을 행사하다 (= exercise/ wield clout)

  `cf` economic clout: 경제적 영향력

- **use A to do B:** B를 하기 위해 A를 사용하다 (= use A for doing B)

  He used his position to get him a job. 그는 자기의 위치를 이용해서 그에게 일자리를 구해주었다.

- **engage in political activities:** 정치활동을 하다 (= do/ conduct/ perform political activities)

- **(be) engaged in:** ~에 종사하다

  He is engaged in teaching. 그는 교직에 종사하고 있다.

2. 여기서 문제는 복잡하고 바쁜 현대사회에서 국민 한 사람 한 사람이 그 정치인을 수시로 만나서 어떤 사람인지 직접 객관적으로 확인할 방법이 없다는 데 있다.

>>> (a) The problem, however, is that the complex and hectic life in modern society makes it hardly possible for the people to find ways to meet one-on-one with the politicians whenever they want so they can size them up in a more direct and objective way.

- **the problem is (that):** 문제는 ~한 것이다

  The problem is, there is no one on my side. 문제는 내 편에 아무도 없다.

- **the complex and hectic life in modern society:** 현대 사회의 복잡하고 바쁜 생활

  `cf` a hectic social life: 매우 바쁜 사회생활

- **make it possible for someone to do:** 아무개가 ~하는 것을 가능하게 하다 (= enable someone to do)

Using the Internet makes it possible to do business at home. 인터넷을 사용하여 집에서 사업을 하는 것이 가능하게 되었다.

- find ways to do: ~을 할 수 있는 방법을 찾다

- meet one-on-one with the politicians: 개인적으로 정치인을 만나다 (= meet the politicians one at a time; on a one-on-one basis; face-to-face; personally; privately; individually)

- meet with someone: (특히 논의를 위해) 아무개를 만나다
I met with him to discuss the problem. 그 문제를 토의하기 위해 그를 만났다.
cf visit with someone: 환담하며 시간을 함께 보내다

- whenever they want: 수시로 (= at any time; at will)

- so (that) they can do: 그들이 ~을 할 수 있도록 (= so as to do; in order to do)

- size up someone/ situation: 아무개를/ 어떤 상황을 평가하다 (= sum up/ judge/ assess someone)

- in a direct and objective way/ manner: 직접적이고 객관적인 방법으로

>>> (b) The problem, however, is that the complex and busy life in modern society prevents the people from finding ways to meet individually with the politicians at any time so as to assess them more directly and objectively.

- prevent someone from doing: 아무개로 하여금 ~을 하지 못하게 하다

- so as to do: ~을 하기 위해

- assess: (사람이나 사물의 특성·자질 등을) 가늠하다 (= judge/ evaluate/ size up)
cf assess the damage/ the extent of/ the impact of: 손해/ ~의 정도/ ~의 영향력을 측정하다

3. 결국 국민들은 그 정치인이 "어떻게 보이느냐"에 좌우되어 그를 지지하고 신뢰하고 표를 던지는 것이 현실이고, 따라서 정치인은 "남들에게 어떻게 보이느냐"에 가장 신경을 쓸 수밖에 없다.

>>> The reality, therefore, is that the decision made by the people to support, trust and vote for any particular politicians is often influenced by how they are perceived by the general public. As a result, the politicians are left with no choice but to concern themselves with the way they appear to other people.

- **the reality is that**: 현실이 ~이다
  The reality is that young people do not want to do hard work. 젊은이들은 힘든 일을 원치 않는 것이 현실이다.

- **vote for someone**: 아무개에 표를 찍다 (= vote in favor of someone)

- **influence the decision to do**: ~하는 결정에 영향을 미치다 (= sway the decision to do)
  cf influence choice/ outcome: 선택/ 결과에 영향을 미치다
  His parents influenced him to go to a medical school. 그의 부모가 그가 의대를 가도록 영향을 미쳤다.

- **how they are perceived/ viewed by the general public**: 일반 대중에 비치는 모습

- **be left with no choice but to do**: ~을 할 수밖에 없다 (= have no choice but to do; cannot help doing; have no choice except to do; cannot stop oneself from doing; have no alternative but to do)
  I was left with no choice but to take the job. 나는 그 일을 택할 수밖에 없었다.

- **concern oneself with**: ~에 신경을 쓰다 (= pay attention to; be interested in)
  Don't concern yourself with her problem. 그녀의 문제에 신경 쓰지 말라.

- **the way they appear to the people**: 사람들에게 보이는 모습 (= public image/ persona)

관련 유용 표현

1. 취직을 하고자 하는 열망은 굉장히 큰데 문제는 그가 영어를 못한다는 것이다.

- 문제는 ~이다: The problem is ~

>>> He is really looking for a job, but the problem is he doesn't speak English.

2. 그와 1대1로 직접 만나고 싶다. 이 사안은 무척 중요해서 그냥 넘어갈 일이 아니기 때문이다.

- 1대1로: one-on-one (= individually)
- 그냥 넘어가다: avoid; evade; overlook

>>> I want to meet one-on-one with him to discuss the issue, which is too important to evade.

핵폭탄 공포

번역과 영작

미국 대도시에서 핵폭탄이 터질 경우 50만 명이 즉사하고 1조 달러의 재산 피해가 발생할 것으로 추산된다. 그 후 방사능 낙진 등으로 수십만이 죽을 것이다. 실제 피해보다 이로 인한 정신적 쇼크는 훨씬 더 클 것이다. 미국만이 아니고 런던, 파리, 베이징, 도쿄 등 세계 주요국 대도시에서 연쇄적으로 이런 일이 벌어진다면 우리가 아는 세상은 사실상 사라질 수 있다.

(미주 한국일보 오피니언 2012.03.28.)

＊ ＊ ＊

Should a nuclear bomb go off in a major city in America, approximately half a million people would die on the spot, with the property damage put at a trillion dollars and hundreds and thousands of more people expected to face a lingering death from radioactive fallout or something.

Moreover, the emotional shock of the explosion would be much greater than that of the actual structural damage itself.

Again, if a series of such explosions should occur in the cosmopolitan cities like London, Paris, Beijing, or Tokyo as well as in America, virtually the whole world as we know it today would be completely wiped out.

해설

1. 미국 대도시에서 핵폭탄이 터질 경우 50만 명이 즉사하고 1조 달러의 재산 피해가 발생할 것으로 추산된다. 그 후 방사능 낙진 등으로 수십만이 죽을 것이다.

>>> Should a nuclear bomb go off in a major city in America, approximately half a million people would die on the spot, with the property damage put at a trillion dollars and hundreds and thousands of more people expected to face a lingering death from radioactive fallout or something (else).

- **should a nuclear bomb go off**: 핵 폭탄이 터질 경우 (= if a nuclear bomb should go off)
- **go off**: 폭발하다 (= explode; detonate; set off)
- **die on the spot**: 즉사하다 (= be killed immediately)
  - **on the spot**: 즉석에서 (= immediately)

- property damage: 재산 피해

- put ~ at: ~으로 추산되다 (= estimate ~ at; assess ~ at)
  His fortune is put at $10 billion. 그의 재산은 100억 달러로 추산된다.

- face lingering death: 오래 앓다가 죽다
  cf (Let's) face it: 싫지만 사실을 사실대로 인정하자/ 받아들이자

- radioactive fallout: 방사능 낙진

- or something (else): 그 밖의 것으로

2. 실제 피해보다 이로 인한 정신적 쇼크는 훨씬 더 클 것이다.

>>> Moreover, the emotional shock of the explosion would be much greater than that of the actual structural damage itself.

- the emotional shock of: ~의 정신적 쇼크 (= the psychological shock)
  - actual damage: 실제 피해

3. 미국만이 아니고 런던, 파리, 베이징, 도쿄 등 세계 주요국 대도시에서 연쇄적으로 이런 일이 벌어진다면 우리가 아는 세상은 사실상 사라질 수 있다.

>>> Again, if a series of such explosions should occur in the cosmopolitan cities like London, Paris, Beijing, or Tokyo as well as in America, virtually the whole world as we know it today would be completely wiped out.

- a series of: 일련의

- **explosions occur**: 폭발이 발생하다, 폭발되다 (= explosions happen/ come/ take place) **cf** **nuclear blast occurs**: 핵폭탄이 터지다
- **cosmopolitan cities**: 세계적 도시 (= the metropolitan area)
- **virtually the whole world as we know it today**: 오늘날 우리가 알고 있는 사실상 전 세계 (= the world as seen through our eyes)
  cf **the world/ city as we know it today**: 오늘날 우리가 알고 있는 세계/ 도시
- **wipe out**: 완전히 흔적을 없애다 (= annihilate/ decimate/ obliterate; reduce ~ to ashes; completely blow up)

관련 유용 표현

1. 화재로 인한 건물 파손은 총 수리비가 5천 달러로 추산된다.

- 화재로 인한 건물 파손: fire damage to a building
- ~의 총 수리비: the total cost of repairing
- ~을 수리하다: repair something
- ~로 추산되다: be estimated to be (= be estimated at)
  - be estimated to be 500 dollars (= comes to 500 dollars)

>>> The total cost of repairing the fire damage to the building is estimated to be 5,000 dollars.

2. 현지인을 대상으로 공공연하게 마약을 팔던 그 마약 밀매자는 추방 당할 처지가 되었다.

- 현지인: the locals
- 마약 밀매자: a drug dealer
- 공공연하게: in public
- 추방: deportation
- (마약 등을) 밀거래하다: traffic in
- ~할 처지가 되다: face something
    - face: (난관)에 부닥치다

    face problems/ difficulty: 문제/ 어려움에 처하다.

    face charge: 고발, 기소 당하다

>>> The drug dealer, who used to traffic in the illegal drugs in public with the locals, now faces deportation.

3

민주주의와 투표

많은 나라에서 총과 펜과 혀가 역사를 바꿔왔다. 그러나 민주주의 제도에 서 표만큼 강력한 것은 없다. 총과 펜과 혀는 커다란 영향력을 가지고 있지만 어느 것도 표만큼 즉각적이고 구체적이지는 않다. 일단 투표로 정해지면 무 엇으로도 바꿀 수 없다. 아무리 힘 센 총과 펜과 혀라도 결과를 뒤집을 순 없 다. 선거가 끝나면 대통령과 국회의원은 현실이 되어 국민 앞에 우뚝 서 있다.

(중앙일보 2012.04.09.)

* * *

In many countries, the gun, the pen and the tongue have changed the course of history; however, there is nothing as powerful as the vote under the democratic system.

Although the gun, pen and tongue carry enormous clout with them, they lack the immediacy and concreteness of the vote.

In the democratic process, for instance, a decision, once reached by vote, is final, i.e. there is absolutely no possibility of reversing it. The gun, pen and tongue, powerful as they may be, cannot overturn the result of voting.

Thus when the election is over, the president and the lawmakers become a reality standing tall before the whole people.

 B 해설

1. 많은 나라에서 총과 펜과 혀가 역사를 바꿔왔다. 그러나 민주주의 제도에서 표만큼 강력한 것은 없다.

>>> In many countries, the gun, the pen and the tongue have changed the course of history. However, there is nothing as powerful as the vote under the democratic system.

• change the course of history: 역사(의 흐름)를 바꾸다

  • the course of history: 역사의 흐름 **cf** the course of life: 인생 행로

• under the democratic system: 민주주의 제도 하에서
  cf under the law/ rule/ term: 법/ 규칙/ 조건에 따라

2. 총과 펜과 혀는 커다란 영향력을 가지고 있다. 하지만 어느 것도 표만큼 즉각적이고 구체적이지는 않다.

> >>> Although the gun, pen and tongue carry enormous clout with them, they lack the immediacy and concreteness of the vote.

- **carry clout:** 힘, 영향력이 있다 (= carry power/ weight)
  cf carry responsibility: 책임을 떠맡다 **have authority:** 권위가 있다
- **lack:** ~이 부족하다, 결핍되다 (= be lacking in)
  He lacks confidence. 그는 자신이 없다.
- **immediacy:** 신속성, 즉각성
- **concreteness:** 구체성

3. 일단 투표로 정해지면 무엇으로도 바꿀 수 없다. 아무리 힘 센 총과 펜과 혀라도 결과를 뒤집을 순 없다.

> >>> In the democratic process, for instance, a decision, once reached by vote, is final, i.e. there is absolutely no possibility of reversing it. The gun, pen and tongue, powerful as they may be, cannot overturn the result of voting.

- **in the democratic process:** 민주주의 과정에서는
- **reach/ make a decision:** ~을 결정하다
- **by vote:** 투표로
- **be final:** 변경할 수 없다 (= be irreversible; ~, period!)
- **there is absolutely no possibility of doing:** ~을 결코 할 수 없다 (= there is no way of doing; it's impossible to do)

- reverse/ overturn/ overrule a decision: 결정을 뒤집다

- powerful as ~ may be: ~이 아무리 강력할지라도 (= although ~ may be powerful)

- overturn/ reverse the result of: ~의 결과를 뒤집다 (= overturn/ reverse the outcome of)

4. 따라서 선거가 끝나면 대통령과 국회의원은 현실이 되어 국민 앞에 우뚝 서 있다.

>>> Thus when the election is over, the president and the lawmakers become a reality standing tall before the whole people.

- be over: ~이 끝나다
  cf It's not over (= It ain't over) until it's over: 아직 끝나지 않았다(두고 봐야 안다).
  Are you finished with the meal? 식사 끝났나?
  Are you done with the paper? 신문 다 봤나?
  World War II ended in 1945. 세계 2차대전은 1945년에 끝났다.

- become a reality: (꿈이 아니라) 현실이 되다

- stand tall: 당당하게 서다 **cf** emerge triumphant: 승리를 거두다

- before the people: 국민 앞에

 관련 유용 표현

1. 정부 관료들은 경기 침체 추세를 역전시킬 방법을 찾는 데 고심하고 있다.

- 정부관료: government officials

- 경기 침체: recession
- 불경기의 추세를 역전시키다: buck the trend of recession
- ~을 하는 방법: ways to do
- ~을 할 수 있는 방법을 알아내다: figure out how to do
- ~에 고심하다: grapple with (= wrestle/ struggle with)

>>> (a) The government officials are grappling with ways to figure out how to buck the trend of the recession

(b) The government is struggling to explore ways to get the country to emerge from the recession.

- ~의 방법을 찾다: explore/ find/ figure out a way to do
- 경기 침체를 벗어나다: emerge from recession (= pull the country out of recession)

2. 일본 정부는 아직도 생존해 계시는 위안부와 관련된 사실을 왜곡함으로써 역사를 바꿀 수 있을 것이라 생각하는가?

- 위안부와 관련된 사실: facts about the comfort women
- 사실을 왜곡하다: distort/ misrepresent/ falsify a fact
- 사실을 왜곡함으로써: by distorting a fact
- 역사를 바꾸다: rewrite history
- ~을 함으로써: by doing ~

>>> Does the Japanese government believe that they can rewrite history by distorting the historical facts about the comfort women, some of whom are still alive in Korea?

4

정치인의 기질

A 번역과 영작

사람마다 기질이 다르다. 그 기질은 타고나는 경우도 있고 인생관 혹은 인생 경험에 의해 결정되기도 한다. 그 기질에 따라 인생항로가 달라지는 경우가 허다하다. 권력에도 그 기질은 반영된다. 대통령직은 법이 정한 권력이 있다. 어떤 대통령이든 제도적으로 부과된 권력은 동일하다. 그러나 그 대통령의 기질에 따라 권력이 행사되는 방식과 결과는 천자만별이다. 그 기질이 우유부단하다면 권력행사도 우유부단하게 될 것이고, 그의 기질이 단호하다면 권력도 단호하게 행사된다. 권력의 기질은 바로 리더의 기질로부터 나온다고 말할 수도 있다.

(중앙일보 2012.07.17.)

* * *

Everyone has their unique character. Some people are born with their personal character, while others have their character formed by how they view their life or by what they go through in their lives.

Every so often the whole course of their life is completely changed by the kind of character that they have.

Moreover, character is reflected in political power as well. For instance, the presidency carries executive power, as stipulated by the constitutional law, with every president being equally vested with the power provided by the system.

However, depending on the president's character, the way power is used and the kinds of results that are yielded vary widely from president to president.

Generally speaking, if the president's character is indecisive, so is the way he exercises his power, and, by the same token, if his character is resolute, the way he exerts his power tends to be resolute as well.

Therefore, it may be safe to assume that the character of power is derived from the leader's character.

 해설

1. 사람마다 기질이 다르다. 그 기질은 타고나는 경우도 있고 인생관 혹은 인생 경험에 의해 결정되기도 한다.

>>> Everyone has their unique character. Some people are born with their personal character, while others have their character formed by how they view their life or by what they go through in their lives.

- their → everyone은 단수형이지만 'his or her' 대신 쓸 수 있는 소유격
- **their unique character:** 그들의 특유한 기질 (= personality; temperament)
- **be born with:** (병, 성격)을 가지고 태어나다
  cf He is born blind/ lucky. 그는 시각장애인으로/ 행운아로 태어났다.
- **form character:** 기질을 형성하다 (= shape/ mold character)
- **how they view their life:** 그들의 인생을 보는 방식 (= by their view of life)
- **what they go through in their lives:** 그들이 생활에서 얻는 경험, 인생관 (= their real-life experience) **cf** **acquired character:** 후천성 기질

2. 그 기질에 따라 인생 항로가 달라지는 경우가 허다하다.

>>> Every so often, (the whole course of) their life is completely changed by the kind of character they have.

- **every so often:** 흔히 (= very often; often times)
- **the course of life:** 인생 항로

3. 권력에도 기질은 반영된다. 대통령직은 법이 정한 권력이 있다. 어느 대통령이든 제도적으로 부과된 권력은 동일하다.

>>> Moreover, character is reflected in political power as well. For instance, the presidency carries executive power, as stipulated by the constitutional law, with every president being equally vested with the power provided by the system.

- **be reflected in:** ~에 반영된다 (= be a sign of~)

- political power: 권력

- the presidency carries executive power as stipulated by the constitutional law 대통령은 헌법에 정해진 대로 행정력을 수행한다 (= the power comes with the presidency; executive power resides in the presidency)

    - carry power: 권력을 갖다 [cf] carry authority: 권위를 갖다

    - executive power: 행정력

    - as stipulated by the constitution: 헌법에 정해진 대로 (= as defined/ mandated by the constitutional law; as authorized by the law; as required by the law)

- be vested with power: 권력이 부여되다 (= power is vested in; power resides in)

4. 그러나 그 대통령의 기질에 따라 권력이 행사되는 방식과 결과는 천차만별이다.

>>> However, depending on the president's character, the way power is used and the kinds of results that are yielded vary widely from president to president.

- depending on: ~에 따라

- the way power is used: 권력이 행사되는 방식 (= the way power is exercised/ wielded/ exerted)

- the kinds of results that are yielded: 나타나는 결과

- yield results: 결과를 초래하다 (= yield/ produce/ bring about results)

- vary (widely) from A to B: A와 B가 (매우) 다르다 (= A and B are different from each other)
  The American accent varies from place to place. 미국식 발음은 곳곳에 따라 다르다.

5. 그 기질이 우유부단하다면 권력행사도 우유부단하게 될 것이고, 그의 기질이 단호하다면 권력도 단호하게 행사된다.

>>> Generally speaking, if the president's character is indecisive, so is the way he exercises his power, and, by the same token, if his character is resolute, the way he exerts his power tends to be resolute as well.

- **generally speaking:** 일반적으로 말하면 (= by and large; in general)
- **be indecisive:** 우유부단하다 (= be inconsistent)
- **, so is~:** ~도 마찬가지다
- **by the same token:** 마찬가지로 (= similarly; for the same reason)
- **be resolute:** 단호하다 (= be determined)
- **tend to do:** ~하는 경향이 있다 (= have a tendency to do)
- **as well:** ~도 (= also)

6. 권력의 기질은 바로 지도자의 기질로부터 나온다고 말할 수도 있다.

>>> Therefore, it may be safe to assume that the character of power is derived from the leader's character.

- **it may be safe to assume/ say that:** ~라고 말할 수 있다 (= we can safely assume that)
- **derive A from B:** B에서 A를 얻다(A comes from B)

1. 미국 어느 곳에 사느냐에 따라서 생활비가 더 들어가거나 덜 들 수 있는데, 샌프란시스코와 뉴욕이 생활비가 제일 많이 드는 곳이다.

- 어디서 ~을 하느냐에 따라서: depending on where
- 생활비가 더 많이 들거나 덜 들 수 있다: the cost of living can be higher or lower
    - 생활비: the cost of living; living expenses; living costs
- 생활비가 제일 많이 드는 곳이다: are the most expensive places to live in

>>> Depending on where you live in America, the cost of living can be higher or lower, with San Francisco and New York being the most expensive cities to live in.

2. 현 대통령의 우유부단한 외교적 행보와 국내 개혁 정책 부진이 선거 패배의 요인으로 꼽힌다.

- 현 대통령: the current/ sitting/ incumbent President
- 우유부단한 외교적 행보: the inconsistent/ indecisive way diplomacy is conducted; the inconsistent conduct of diplomacy
- 국내 개혁 정책 부진: a long delay in carrying out a reform policy in Korea
- 패배의 요인으로 꼽힌다: be presumed/ alleged to be the determining factor in a total failure to win the election

>>> The inconsistent way diplomacy is conducted by the sitting President plus a long delay in carrying out a reform policy in Korea is alleged to be the determining factor in a total failure (to win the election.)

5

세법 개정

  번역과 영작

내년 세법 개정안 손질이 막바지에 왔다. 다음 달 초 정부안이 발표된다. 말은 무성했지만 올해도 각종 감면 제도가 확 줄어들긴 어려울 전망이다. 경기도 안 좋고, 반발도 크기 때문이다.

(중앙일보 2012.07.27.)

* * *

The process of tweaking the tax system for the coming year is nearly complete, with the revised government version set to be released at the beginning of next month.

Although there has been wild speculation about the reform of the tax law, the kinds of tax-deductible expenses that may be claimed this year (when the tax returns are filed) are not expected to be drastically reduced due largely to the sluggish economic conditions, plus strong public opposition to the radical overhaul of the tax code.

1. 내년 세법 개정안 손질이 막바지에 왔다. 다음 달 초 정부안이 발표된다.

>>> The process of tweaking the tax system for the coming year is nearly complete, with the revised government version set to be released at the beginning of next month.

- the process of doing: ~하는 과정
- tweak the tax system: 세법을 개정하다
    - tweak: 개정하다 (= overhaul; reform; revise)
    - the tax system: 조세 제도 (= the tax law/ code)
- be nearly complete: 거의 끝나다 (= near completion; be almost done)
- the revised government version: 정부의 개정안
- be set to do: ~하기로 예정되다 (= be slated to do)
- release: ~를 공개 발표하다 (= announce; unveil; publish)

2. 말은 무성했지만 올해도 각종 감면 제도가 확 줄어들긴 어려울 전망이다. 경기도 안 좋고, 반발도 크기 때문이다.

>>> Although there has been wild speculation about the reform of the tax law, the kinds of tax-deductible expenses that may be claimed this year (when the tax returns are filed) are not expected to be drastically reduced due largely to the sluggish economic conditions, plus strong public opposition to the radical overhaul of the tax code.

- **there is (wild) speculation about:** ~에 관한 (온갖) 추측이 난무하다 (= speculation abounds about/ speculation runs rife/ rampant as to; speculation that ~ has been bubbling away/ up)
- **the revision of the tax system:** 세제 개정 (= tax reform)
- **claim the kinds of tax-deductible expenses:** 각종 세금 공제 비용을 청구하다
   claim compensation/ pension/ damage: 보상금/ 연금/ 손해배상을 청구하다
- **file the tax return:** 세금 보고를 하다
   file a claim/ lawsuit: ~을 청구하다/ 소송을 제기하다
- **reduce expenses:** 비용을 감축하다 (= cut/ curtail expenses)
- **due (largely) to:** (주로) ~때문에 (= mainly because of)
- **sluggish economic conditions:** 부진한 경제 상황 (= sagging/ troubled/ stagnant economic conditions)
- **plus:** ~과 함께 (= coupled with; combined with)
- **find ways to do:** ~을 할 수 있는 방법을 찾다 (= explore/ figure out ways to do)
- **opposition to:** ~의 반대 (= be against/ object to)
- **radical/ complete overhaul of:** ~의 근본적인 정비 (= complete/ radical/ drastic change of)
- **reform the tax code:** 세금 제도를 개정하다 (= revise the tax code)

C 관련 유용 표현

1. 금년 대통령 선거에서 누가 당선되느냐에 관해 추측이 무성하다.

- 선거에서 당선되다: win an election

- 대통령 선거: the presidential election
- 에 관해 추측하다: there is speculation about

>>> There is a great deal of speculation about who will win the presidential election this year.

2. 지금까지 이 세상에서 위대한 업적 치고 열정 없이 이루어진 것은 하나도 없다고 우리는 확실하게 단언할 수 있다.

- 열정 없이: without passion
- ~이 이루어진 것은 하나도 없다: nothing has been accomplished
- 확실하게: absolutely
- ~라고 단언하다: affirm that

>>> We may affirm absolutely that nothing great in the world has been accomplished without passion. (Hegel)

3. 이번에 개정되는 세법 시행규칙은 3월 4일부터 공포돼 시행된다.

- 개정된 세법: the revised version of the tax system
- 3월 4일부터 시행되다: be effective from March 4th (= take effect/ come into effect/ be enforced from March 4th)

>>> The government has announced that the revised version of the tax system is effective from March 4th.

6

삶과 투자

삶은 투자의 연속이다. 살아오면서 무엇에 투자했는지가 '오늘의 당신'이 누구인지를 말해주고, 앞으로 어디에 투자할 지가 '미래의 당신'을 결정한다. 투자에는 리스크가 상존한다. 특히 지금은 예측이 불가능한 사회가 됐다. 이제 당신은 무엇에 어떻게 투자해 당신의 삶을 더 나은 상태로 만들 것인가.

(동아일보 2012.02.26.)

* * *

Life often involves making a series of investments. What you have invested in up until now says something about who you are now, and what you will invest in from now on will determine who you will be in the future.

However, there are always risks involved in the investments, especially at this particular time when it is almost impossible to make any correct predictions.

If so, what would you invest in now, and how would you make solid investments to ensure that you will be better off than now?

 B 해설

1. 삶은 투자의 연속이다.

>>> Life often involves making a series of investments. (= Life often involves making a succession of investments.)

- involve doing: ~하는 것이 포함되다, ~을 하게 되다, ~을 할 필요가 있다
- make investments in: 투자하다 (= invest in)
  cf You are often tempted to make a series of investments during your lifetime.
    - be tempted to do: ~을 하고 싶은 유혹을 느끼다
    - during your lifetime: 당신 생애에서
  cf invest in clothes/ education: 옷/ 교육에 돈을 쓰다

2. 살아오면서 무엇에 투자했는지가 '오늘의 당신'이 누구인지를 말해주고, 앞으로 어디에 투자할 지가 '미래의 당신'을 결정한다.

>>> What you have invested in up until now says something about who you are now, and what you will invest in from now on will determine who you will be in the future.

- **what you have invested in:** 당신이 투자해 온 것

- **up until now:** 지금까지 (= so far; thus far)

- **say something about who you are:** 당신이 누구인지 말해주다

  - **who you are:** 현재의 당신

- **from now on:** 지금부터

- **determine who you will be in the future:** 미래의 당신을 결정하다

3. 투자에는 리스크가 상존한다. 특히 지금은 예측이 불가능한 사회가 됐다.

>>> However, there are always risks involved in the investments, especially at this particular time when it is almost impossible to make any correct predictions.

- **There are risks involved in the investments:** 투자에는 리스크가 있다 (= There are risks associated with the investments; Risks come with the investments; The investments have their own inherent risks.)

  - **risks come with:** ~에는 위험이 있다

- **at this particular time when:** 특히 ~한 현재에는

- **make predictions:** 예측하다

4. 이제 당신은 무엇에 어떻게 투자해 당신의 삶을 더 나은 상태로 만들 것인가.

>>> If so, what would you invest in now, and how would you make solid investments to ensure that you will be better off than now?

- **if so:** 그렇다면 (= if that is the case)

- **make solid investments**: 확실한 투자를 하다

- **to ensure that**: ~을 확실히 하기 위해 (= to make sure that)

- **be better off than now**: 지금 보다 더 잘 살다

관련 유용 표현

1. 소득도 높고 처우도 좋지만 그 직업의 단점은 야근을 하는 것이다.

- 처우: fringe benefits
- ~의 단점: the disadvantage of (= the downside of)
- ~을 하는 것이 포함되다: involve doing
- 야근: work at night (be on night duty)

> >>> Despite the good pay with fringe benefits, the disadvantage of the job is that it involves working at night.

  cf I work a 12-hour shift: 난 12시간씩 교대하면서 일한다.
  cf I work night shift: 나는 밤 교대를 한다.

2. 경찰은 아직 그 여성의 정확한 사인을 밝히지 못했다. 자칫 사건이 미궁에 빠질까 유족은 두려워하고 있다.

- 사인을 밝히다: determine the cause of death

• 미궁에 빠지다: be veiled/ shrouded in mystery

>>> The police have not been able to determine the cause of her death yet, and so the family of the victim are concerned that the circumstance surrounding her death may be shrouded in mystery.

고급 번역과 영작 연습

⑦ 청년 실업

번역과 영작

우리나라의 청년(15~29세) 실업자는 약 27만명으로 실업률로 따지면 6.7%에 달한다. 공식통계에 잡히지 않는 청년 무직자를 포함하면 청년 실업자는 100만명에 달할 것이라고 정부는 추산하고 있다. 다시 말해 우리의 미래를 짊어지고 갈 청년 네댓 명 중 하나는 경제 활동을 하지 않고 있다는 것이다. 이같은 상황을 개선하는 데 가장 효과적인 수단으로 창업이 꼽히고 있다. 하지만 현실은 어둡다.

(조선일보 2012.11.27.)

* * *

Approximately 270 thousand young Koreans in the 15-to-29 age bracket are now out of work, making up 6.7% of the jobless rate in Korea.

The government, however, puts the total number of the unemployed youth at one million, including those excluded from the official statistics

- in other words, one in four or five young Koreans, who will eventually embrace the future of our country, has yet to get an opportunity to participate in the economic activities.

Under the circumstances, starting up in business is considered to be the most effective way to improve the job situation in Korea, but, as things stand, the reality now looks rather grim.

 B 해설

1. 우리나라의 청년(15~29세) 실업자는 약 27만 명으로 실업률로 따지면 6.7%에 달한다.

>>> (a) Approximately 270 thousand young Koreans in the 15-to-29 age bracket are now out of work, making up 6.7% of the jobless rate in Korea.

- **approximately:** 대략 (= roughly; almost; nearly)
- **Koreans in the 15-to-29 age bracket:** 15세에서 29세에 해당하는 한국 사람
    - **bracket:** 집단 (= group; range; category)
- **be out of work:** 실직 중이다 (= be jobless; be without a job; join the ranks of the unemployed) **cf** I'm between jobs: 직장을 잃고 지금 찾는 중이다.
- **make up** (~%): (~퍼센트)에 해당하다 (= represent; constitute; amount to; account for)
- **the jobless rate:** 실업률 (= the unemployment rate)

>>> (b) Unemployment remaining at 270 thousands among the young Koreans in the 15-to-29 age group accounts for 6.7% of the jobless rate in Korea.

- **unemployment remains at**: 실업자 수가 ~로 남아 있다
- **account for**: ~에 해당하다 (= make up; represent; constitute)

>>> (c) The number of the unemployed Koreans in the 15-to-29 age category roughly stands at 270 thousands, or 6.7% of the jobless rate, in Korea.

- **the number of**: ~의 수
- **stand at**: (~의 수량에) 달하다
- **, or**: 즉(동격을 가리키는 표현으로)

2. 공식 통계에 잡히지 않는 청년 무직자를 포함하면 청년 실업자는 100만 명에 달할 것으로 정부는 추산하고 있다.

>>> The government, however, puts the total number of the unemployed youth at one million, including those excluded from the official statistics.

- **put/ estimate A at something**: A를 ~으로 추산하다
- **those excluded from**: ~에서 누락된 이들 (= those missing from)
- **the official statistics**: 공식 통계

3. 다시 말해 우리의 미래를 짊어지고 갈 청년 네댓 명 중 하나는 경제 활동을 하지 않고 있다는 것이다.

>>> - in other words, one in four or five young Koreans, who will eventually embrace the future of our country, has yet to get an opportunity to participate in the economic activities.

- in other words: 다시 말해 (= to put it another way; that is to say; that is)

- one in four: 넷 중 하나 **cf** nine out of ten: 열 중 아홉

- embrace the future of our country: 우리 나라의 미래를 받아들이다

cf take on the challenge of our future: 우리의 미래의 도전을 떠맡다
  assume responsibility for our future: 우리의 미래를 책임지다
  take charge of our future: 우리의 미래를 장악하다
  carry our future: 우리의 미래를 이끌고 가다

- participate in the economic activities: 경제 활동에 참여하다 (= take part in the job markets)

4. 이 같은 상황을 개선하는 데 가장 효과적인 수단으로 창업이 꼽히고 있다. 하지만 현실은 어둡다.

>>> Under the circumstances, starting up in business is considered to be the most effective way to improve the job situation in Korea, but, as things stand, the reality now looks rather grim.

- under the circumstances: 이러한 상황에서 (= given the circumstances)

- set up (in) business: 창업하다 (= start up a business)
  cf go out of business: 폐업하다

- **the most effective way to do:** ~을 하는 데 가장 유효한 방법

- **improve the job situation:** 일자리 상황을 개선하다

- **as things stand:** 현 상황에서는 (= as it stands; as matters stand; as it is; to all appearances; for the way things are/ stand)

C 관련 유용 표현

1. 아시아인이 미국 인구의 5%를 차지한다. 결코 작은 수치가 아님에도 불구하고 아직도 아이사인이 미국 사회에 적극 동참한다고 보기는 어렵다.

- 차지하다: account for (= make up; represent; comprise)

- 결코 아니다: by no means (= not ~ at all)

- 적극 동참하다: get actively involved in (= actively participate in; take an active part in; get on board)

> >>> Asians account for 5% of the U.S. population, which is by no means a small proportion. Still, they can hardly be considered to get actively involved in American life.

2. 현재 한국에 거주하는 외국인 수는 전체 인구의 약 3%로 추산된다. 한국사람들은 국수주의를 버려야 할 때가 되었다.

- 현재: as of now

- 한국에 거주하는 외국인: the foreign residents in Korea

- ~로 추산되다: be estimated to be/ at

- 국수주의: nationalism

- ~할 때가 되다: It's high time you did (= It's time to do; It's time you did)

>>> As of now the number of the foreign residents in Korea is estimated to be approximately 3% of the whole population. Hence, it's high time Koreans curbed nationalism.

8

일광 절약

번역과 영작

미국에서 일광 절약 시간(서머 타임) 개념을 처음 생각해 낸 사람은 "일찍 일어나면 건강에도 좋고 돈도 벌며 현명해진다"라는 격언을 남긴 벤저민 프랭클린으로 알려져 있다. 그러나 이 제도가 법적으로 시행된 것은 제1차대전이 한창이던 1918년이다. 독일이 연료를 아낀다는 명분으로 1916년 이를 시작하자 유럽 전체가 그 뒤를 따랐고 미국도 이를 본받은 것이다. 그러다 전쟁이 끝나면서 폐지되고 말았다. 그 후 20여년이 지나 제2차대전이 터지자 같은 이유로 다시 시작됐다.

(미주 한국일보 2012.03.14.)

＊ ＊ ＊

Benjamin Franklin, who left behind a legacy of the maxim that "Early to bed, early to rise makes you healthy, wealthy and wise," is known to have been the first American to come up with the concept of daylight saving time.

However, it was at the height of the World War I in 1918 that the daylight saving time was officially implemented.

In 1916 Germany first adopted the new time system, ostensibly to save energy, followed by the entire European countries, and later the U.S. followed suit as well.

The use of the daylight saving time, however, was discontinued with the end of the war, but, again for reasons of energy conservation, it was resumed following the outbreak of the Second World War after a 20-year hiatus.

 B 해설

1. 미국에서 일광 절약 시간(서머 타임) 개념을 처음 생각해 낸 사람은 "일찍 일어나면 건강에도 좋고 돈도 벌며 현명해진다"라는 격언을 남긴 벤저민 프랭클린으로 알려져 있다.

>>> Benjamin Franklin, who left behind a legacy of the maxim that "Early to bed, early to rise makes you healthy, wealthy and wise," is known to have been the first American to come up with the concept of daylight saving time.

• leave behind: ~을 뒤에 남기고 죽다
• a legacy of the maxim: 격언의 유물/ 유산

- **be known to do:** ~하는 것으로 알려지다

- **the first to do:** ~을 한 최초의 사람

- **come up with:** (아이디어 등을) 생각해 내다 (= be credited with)
  He is always good at coming up with new ideas of doing things. 그는 항상 어떤 일을 하는데 새로운 아이디어를 제시하는 재능이 있다.

- **the concept of daylight saving time (DST):** 일광 절약 시간의 개념
  cf We are on DST now. 요즘 일광절약 시간 중이다.

2. 이 제도가 법적으로 시행된 것은 제1차대전이 한창이던 1918년이다.

>>> … it was at the height of the World War I in 1918 that the daylight saving time was officially implemented.

- **it …. that:** '1918년 제1차대전'을 강조한 구문 → it … that의 강조문
- **at the height of:** ~의 절정에 (= at the peak of)
- **officially implement:** 공식적으로 (정책, 제도 등을) 시행하다 (= adopt; introduce)
  - **implement:** (계획, 정책, 추천, 제도 등을) 시행하다
  The government has implemented the new economic policy. 정부는 새로운 정책을 시행했다.

3. 독일이 연료를 아낀다는 명분으로 1916년 이를 시작하자 유럽 전체가 그 뒤를 따랐고 미국도 이를 본받은 것이다.

>>> In 1916 Germany first adopted the new time system, ostensibly to save energy, followed by the entire European countries, and later the U.S. followed suit as well.

- adopt a system: (제도, 정책, 방법) 등을 채택하다

- ostensibly to do: ~을 한다는 명분으로

- , followed by: ~가 그 뒤를 따르다

- follow suit: 남이 한대로 따라 하다 (= do the same as someone else has done)

4. 그러다 전쟁이 끝나면서 폐지되고 말았다. 20여년이 지나 제2차대전이 터지자 같은 이유로 다시 시작됐다.

>>> The use of the daylight saving time, however, was discontinued with the end of the war, but, again for reasons of energy conservation, it was resumed following the outbreak of the Second World War after a 20-year hiatus.

- the use of: ~의 사용

- discontinue: ~을 중단하다
  They discontinued the use of imported products. 그들은 외제품 사용을 중단했다.

- with the end of: ~이 끝나면서 (= when ~ is over)

- for reasons of energy conservation: 에너지 절약 때문에 (= for the purpose of saving energy)

- following the outbreak of the Second World War 제2차대전이 발생하자
  (= when the Second World War broke out)
  cf outbreak of disease: 질병 발생

- resume: ~을 다시 시작하다
  Students resumed a demonstration against the government after police left. 학생들은 경찰이 떠나자 반정부 시위를 다시 시작했다.

- after a 20-year hiatus: 20년 간 중단 된 후 (= after an interval of 20 years)

1. 나의 친한 친구 한 명이 폐암으로 투병하다 죽으면서 그의 아내와 어린 자녀들이 지금 생계를 이어가기 위해 고군분투하고 있다는 소식을 들으니 매우 가슴 아프다.

- 폐암으로 투병하다 죽다: die battling against lung cancer (= die from lung cancer)
- ~을 하고자 애쓰다, 고군분투하다: struggle to do
- 생계를 유지하다: eke out a living (= get by)
- ~을 듣고 가슴 아프게 생각하다: it's heartbreaking to hear that

>>> It's heartbreaking to hear that one of my close friends, who died battling against lung cancer, left behind his wife and small children, who are now struggling to eke out a living.

2. 중국 공산당이 1980년 9월 25일 인구증가 억제를 위해 채택한 한 자녀 정책은 35년 만에 폐지 수순을 밟게 됐다.

- 중국 공산당: the Chinese Communist Party
- 인구증가 억제를 위해: as a way of controlling population growth
- as a way of doing: ~을 하기 위해
- 한 자녀 정책을 채택하다: adopt one-child policy
- 35년 만에: 35 years after it was first initiated
    - initiate policy/ system: 정책, 제도를 처음 시작하다
- (정책/ 제도 등) 폐기 수순을 밟게 되다: be about to abolish/ repeal/ end/ scrap a policy/ system

>>> The Chinese Communist Party, which adopted one-child policy on September 25, 1980 as a way of controlling population growth, is about to get the system abolished 35 years after it was implemented.

Part 2

경제

자녀를 위한 과소비

A   번역과 영작

    한국의 젊은 부모들은 한 자녀만을 갖는 게 일반화되면서 아들딸을 '왕자'와 '공주'로 키우듯 돈을 쏟아 붓고 있다. 아이들 키우는 일이라면 자기 소득 정도나 재산 규모를 아랑곳하지 않는 세태가 돼버렸다. 이런 터무니없는 과소비 풍조는 유아·아동복, 기저귀, 침대로 범위를 넓혀가더니 이제는 30만원대 하는 유아용 수입 딸랑이로까지 확대됐다. 아이 한 명 키우는데 부모와 할아버지 할머니 외할아버지 외할머니까지 지갑을 열어야 할 지경이다.

(조선닷컴 2012.03.29.)

* * *

    With the young Korean couples generally choosing to have only one child, they spare no expenses to raise their kids the way a prince or a princess is brought up.

    Such is the reality that, when it comes to looking after their kids, they are more than happy to do everything possible, regardless of what their income level or financial status is.

The undesirable trend towards such conspicuous consumption has now got to the point where they expand their purchase of the baby items beyond baby clothes, diapers and cradles to include the imported toy bells each priced at as high as $300.

As a result, the babies' grandparents and maternal grandparents as well as their parents all find themselves in a situation where they feel obligated to dig into their pockets to rear just one child.

 해설

1. 한국의 젊은 부모들은 한 자녀 갖는 게 일반화되면서 아들딸을 '왕자'와 '공주'로 키우듯 돈을 쏟아 붓고 있다.

>>> With the young Korean couples generally choosing to have only one child, they spare no expenses to raise their kids the way a prince or a princess is brought up.

• **with someone choosing to do**: 아무개가 ~하길 택하면서

• **choose to do**: ~하기를 택하다

• **spare no expenses to do/ in doing**: ~을 하는 데 돈을 아끼지 않다 (= splurge ~on;

lavishly spend on ~; splash out on ~; spend money like water; spend money like there is no tomorrow; do not skimp/ stint on ~)

- **raise a child:** 아이를 키우다 (= bring up/ rear a child)
- **the way a prince is brought up:** 왕자를 키우듯 (= the way a prince is raised)
- **the way something is done:** ~이 이루어지듯이

2. 아이들 키우는 일이라면 자기 소득 정도나 재산 규모를 아랑곳하지 않는 세태가 돼버렸다.

>>> Such is the reality that, when it comes to looking after their kids, they are more than happy to do everything possible, regardless of what their income level or financial status is.

- **such is the reality ~:** ~현실이 ~할 정도이다
- **when it comes to doing:** ~을 하는 일이라면
  When it comes to doing repairs, I'm all thumbs. 수리하는 것이라면 나는 형편 없다.
- **look after someone:** 아무개를 돌보다 (= provide for/ care for/ take care of)
- **be happy to do:** ~을 기꺼이 하다 (= be willing to do)
- **do everything possible:** 할 수 있는 것은 다 하다 (= do everything one can; do everything humanly possible to do)
  cf **They want all the best for their children.** 그들은 자녀에게 최고를 주고 싶다.
- **regardless of:** ~에 상관 없이 (= irrespective of)
- **income level:** 수입 정도 (= the amount of money one makes)
- **financial status:** 재정상태 (= financial position)

3. 이런 터무니없는 과소비 풍조는 유아·아동복, 기저귀, 침대로 범위를 넓혀가더니 이제는 30만원대 하는 유아용 수입 딸랑이로까지 확대됐다.

> >>> The undesirable trend towards such conspicuous consumption has now got to the point where they expand their purchase of the baby items beyond baby clothes, diapers and cradles to include the imported toy bells each priced at as high as $300.

- **the undesirable trend towards**: 바람직하지 않은 ~의 풍조

- **conspicuous consumption**: 과소비

- **get to the point where**: ~하는 지점까지 도달하다

- **expand their purchase of**: ~의 구매를 확대하다

- **baby items**: 유아용품 (= baby products/ goods)

- **expand A beyond B to include C**: A를 B 이상으로 확대하여 C까지 포함시키다
  expand <u>their purchase of the baby items</u> beyond <u>baby clothes, diapers and cradles</u>
                  A   B
  to include <u>the imported toy bells</u> (= their purchase of the baby items extended
                   C
  beyond clothes, diapers and cradles to include the imported toy bells)
  cf Their shopping list includes C as well as B

- **the imported toy bells each priced at as high as $300**: 한 개에 300불이나 가는 수입 딸랑이 (= the imported toy bells selling for as much as $300 apiece)

4. 아이 한 명 키우는데 부모와 할아버지 할머니 외할아버지 외할머니까지 지갑을 열어야 할 지경이다.

>>> As a result, the babies' grandparents and maternal grandparents as well as their parents all find themselves in a situation where they feel obligated to dig into their pockets to rear just one child.

- **find oneself in a situation where:** ~을 하는 상황에 처하다 (= be (put) in a situation in which; in this situation; under the circumstances)
- **feel obligated to do:** ~해야 한다고 생각하다
- **dig into one's pocket to do:** ~하기 위해서 돈을 쓰다 (= dig down to do; put one's hand into one's pocket to do; spend money on)
  cf contribute money to political fund: 정치 자금에 기부하다
  cf chip in: 돈을 걷어 모으다, 각출하다
- **rear one child:** 아기 하나를 키우다 (= raise; look after; take care of; care for; nurture one child)

관련 유용 표현

1. 수입도 변변치 않으면서 그 여성은 쇼핑을 가서 흥청망청 돈을 물 쓰듯 했다.

- 수입도 변변치 않으면서: despite her modest income
- 쇼핑을 가서 흥청망청 돈을 쓰다: go on a shopping spree
- 돈을 물 쓰듯 하다: spend money like water (= like there is no tomorrow)

>>> Despite her modest income, the woman went on a shopping spree, spending money like water.

2. 문제가 많은 그들의 부부관계는 이혼으로 끝날 지경에까지 이르렀다.

- 문제가 많은 그들의 부부관계: their troubled marital relationship
- 이혼으로 끝나다: end in divorce
- ~할 지경에까지 이르다: have got to the point where

>>> Their troubled marital relationship has got to the point where their marriage is bound to end in divorce

여성의 경제활동

번역과 영작

지난 2008년에 나온 통계에 의하면 여자의 기대수명은 83세이고 남성의 기대수명은 76세라고 한다. 여성이 남성보다 7세가 높다. 그러나 50세 이상 여성 인구의 경제활동을 살펴보면 다소 암울하다. 통계자료에 의하면 50세 이상 남성 인구의 비경제 활동은 29.5%인데 비해 여성은 이보다 높은 57.8%이다. 경제적으로 그만큼 취약하면서도 7년 이상을 혼자 살아야 한다. 즉, 그만큼 돈이 더 필요하다는 것이다.

(미주 한국일보 2010.07.07.)

* * *

Statistics released back in 2008 indicates that the women, who were expected to live to the age of 83, would live 7 years longer than the men, who would live to be 76.

However, a close examination of the economic activities done by the women aged over 50 shows rather a gloomy picture of their employment status.

According to the statistical data, 57.8% of the women were economically inactive, much higher than 29.5% of the men in the same age group.

Thus the women, who are economically so disadvantaged, still have to live 7 more years all on their own, which means they need to have that much more money set aside for their longer life.

 해설

1. 지난 2008년에 나온 통계에 의하면 여자의 기대수명은 83세이고 남성의 기대수명은 76세 라고 한다. 여성이 남성보다 7세가 높다.

>>> Statistics released back in 2008 indicates that the women, who were expected to live to the age of 83, would live 7 years longer than the men, who would live to 76.

- **release statistics**: 통계를 내놓다
- **statistics indicates that**: 통계에 따르면 (= statistics shows/ reveals/ suggests that; according to the statistics)
- **be expected to do**: ~하기로 기대되다
- **live to the age of 83**: 83세까지 살다 (= live to be 83)

2. 그러나 50세 이상 여성 인구의 경제활동을 살펴보면 다소 암울하다.

>>> However, a close examination of the economic activities done by the women aged over 50 shows rather a gloomy picture of their employment status.

- **an examination indicates that:** 살펴보면 ~이 나타나다 (= an examination suggests/ shows/ reveals that)
- **do economic activities:** 경제활동을 하다 (= do/ perform economic activities)
- **a woman aged over 50:** 50이 넘은 여성 (= a woman over the age of 50; a woman (aged) over 50; a woman age 50 plus)
- **show a gloomy picture of:** ~의 암울한 모습을 보이다
- **employment status:** 고용 상태

3. 통계자료에 의하면 50세 이상 남성 인구의 비경제 활동은 29.5%인데 비해 여성은 이보다 높은 57.8%이다.

>>> According to the statistical data, 57.8% of the women were economically inactive, much higher than 29.5% of the men in the same age group.

- **according to the statistical data:** 통계자료에 의하면 (= based on the statistical data; statistical data shows)
- **be economically inactive:** 경제적으로 비활동적이다 (= be out of work)
- **the men in the same age group:** 같은 연령대의 남자

4. 경제적으로 그만큼 취약하면서도 7년 이상을 혼자 살아야 한다. 즉, 그만큼 돈이 더 필요하다는 것이다.

> >>> Thus the women, who are economically so disadvantaged, still have to live 7 more years all on their own, which means they need to have that much more money set aside for their longer life.

- **be economically disadvantaged:** 경제적으로 불리한 조건 하에 놓이다 (= suffer an economic disadvantage; be put at an economic disadvantage)
- **the woman … live 7 more years all on their own** (= the woman outlive the men by 7 years)
- **live on one's own:** 혼자 살다 (= live alone)
- **, which means:** (앞 내용은) ~를 뜻한다 (= , meaning⋯ ; which is one's cue to do; which is why)
- **one's cue to do:** ~하라는 신호
- **have that much more money set aside for their longer life:** 그들의 보다 긴 삶을 위해 돈을 마련해 두다
- **that much more money:** 그만큼 더 많은 돈
- **set aside:** (돈, 시간 등을) 마련해두다 (= save)

관련 유용 표현

1. 비행기 잔해를 면밀히 검토한 결과 그 항공기 추락은 조종사의 과실로 확인되었다.

- 비행기의 잔해: the wreckage of a plane
- ~의 면밀한 검토: a close examination of
- 항공기의 추락: the plane crash
- 조종사의 과실이 원인이다: be caused by pilot error
- ~으로 확인되다: confirm that

>>> A close examination of the wreckage of the plane confirmed that the plane crash was caused by pilot error.

2. 경제적으로 어려운 시기에 많은 소규모 사업체들이 폐업을 하는데 이는 경제가 곧 회복하지 않으면 수천 명의 일자리가 사라질 위험에 처해 있음을 의미한다.

- 경제적으로 어려운 시기: in this time of economic difficulty
- 소규모 사업체: small businesses
- 폐업하다: go out of business (= business goes under/ goes belly up/ goes south)
- 경제가 회복되다: see the quick turnaround in our economy; see the economic recovery
- 일자리가 사라질 위험에 처하다: jobs are on the line
    - be on the line: (job, future 등이) 위태롭다

>>> In this time of economic difficulty, many small businesses are going out of business, which means that thousands of jobs are on the line unless we see quick turnaround in our economy.

11

덴마크의 노조 지향

덴마크인들은 자신들을 우스개 소리로 표현할 때 '2명만 모이면 노조를 만드는 국민'이라고 말한다. 모든 직장인들이 노조에 가입한다. 단체 활동을 좋아하는 것이 덴마크인의 특성이기도 하다. 단체에 가입하지 않은 사람은 국민 100명당 2명 정도에 불과한 것으로 나타나 있다. 그러면 이 노조가 기업주와 사사건건 부딪치느냐 하면 전혀 그렇지가 않다. "국가가 잘되는 길이 회사가 잘되는 길이다. 회사가 잘되면 나도 잘되기 마련이다." 이것이 덴마크인들의 사고방식이다.

(미주 한국일보 2012.03.28.)

＊ ＊ ＊

The Danes often joke that they are the kind of people that always get unionized whenever there is a gathering of no more than two people, that is, in Denmark almost all the workers join the unions.

The Danes are thus characterized as being fond of doing the group activities. For instance, only 2 out of 100 Danes are shown to opt out of any types of groups.

One may then wonder if the union members and the employers don't ever clash with each other over every single issue.

But that won't happen because they get into the mindset that what is good for the nation is good for the companies and what is good for the companies is also good for themselves.

 해설

1. 덴마크인들은 자신들을 우스개 소리로 표현할 때 '2명만 모이면 노조를 만드는 국민'이라고 말한다. 모든 직장인들이 노조에 가입한다.

>>> The Danes often joke that they are the kind of people that always get unionized whenever there is a gathering of no more than two people, that is, in Denmark almost all the workers join the unions.

- **joke that:** ~라고 농담을 하다 (= say jokingly that; say with tongue in cheek that)
- **be the kind of people that:** ~하는 국민이다
- **a gathering of two people:** 두 사람의 모임 (= two people getting together)
- **be/ get unionized:** 노조를 만들다 (= join the union)

2. 단체 활동을 좋아하는 것이 덴마크인의 특성이기도 하다.

>>> The Danes are thus characterized as being fond of doing the group activities.

- **be characterized as (being):** ~라고 특징 지우다 (= characterize A as B)
- **be fond of doing:** ~하기를 좋아하다 (= like to do)
- **group activities:** 단체 활동

3. 단체에 가입하지 않은 사람은 국민 100명당 2명 정도에 불과한 것으로 나타나 있다.

>>> For instance, only 2 out of 100 Danes are shown to opt out of any types of groups.

- **only 2 out of 100 Danes:** 100명의 덴마크인 중 2명 (= of 100 Danes 2 only; only 2 in 100 Danes; 2 in every 100 Danes)
- **be shown to do:** ~을 하는 것으로 나타나다
- **opt out of:** ~에 참여하지 않기로 하다 (= choose not to join)
  cf opt in to: ~의 단체에 가입하다

4. 그러면 이 노조가 기업주와 사사건건 부딪치느냐,

>>> One may then wonder if the union members and the employers don't ever clash with each other over every single issue.

- **one may wonder if people don't ever clash with each other over:** 아무개가 ~에 대해 충돌하지나 않을까 궁금할 지도 모른다

- **one may wonder if**: ~인지 궁금할 것이다 (= you/ people may wonder if)
- **clash with someone over**: ~때문에 아무개와 부딪치다 (= be on a collision course with someone over; collide with someone over; disagree with someone over/ on/ about; be in dispute with someone over; argue with someone about; be at odds with someone over; be in conflict with someone over)
- **over every single issue**: 사사건건 ~에 대해 (= on/ about single issue)

5. 전혀 그렇지가 않다. "국가가 잘되는 길이 회사가 잘되는 길이다. 회사가 잘되면 나도 잘되기 마련이다." 이것이 덴마크인들의 사고방식이다.

>>> But that won't happen because they get into the mindset that what is good for the nation is good for the companies and what is good for the companies is also good for themselves.

- **that won't happen**: 그런 일은 없다 (= not at all; that's highly unlikely; that's not the case)
- **get into mindset that**: ~한 사고방식을 갖다 (= have the mentality that)
- **what is good for A is good for B**: A에게 좋으면 B에게 좋다
- **because they get into the mindset that**: 왜냐하면 그들은 ~한 사고방식을 갖고 있기 때문에 (= because of the mentality of the people, who believe that; because they have a "…" mentality).
  cf They are in a win-win situation. 그들은 서로가 득이 되는 상황에 있다.

관련 유용 표현

1. 나의 전처도 초청받은 결혼식에 내가 참석을 해야 할까?

- 나의 전처: my ex
- 결혼식에 초청 받다: receive an invite to a wedding
- 결혼식에 참석하다: attend a wedding
- ~을 해야 할까? : I wonder if/ whether

>>> **I wonder if I should attend the wedding, to which my ex has also received an invite/ invitation.**

2. 아내가 남편에게 아이와 놀아주길 바라는데도 십중팔구 그 남편은 주말에 집에 없다.

- 십중팔구: as likely as not; it's more than likely that; nine times out of ten; seldom
- 주말에: on weekends
- 집에 없다: never stay (at) home
- 아이와 놀아주다: spend time with their kids

>>> **Some husbands seldom stay home on weekends, although their wives expect them to spend time with their kids.**

외국 기업의 투자 기피

A

번역과 영작

외국 기업이 국내 직접투자를 꺼리는 것은 우리나라의 투자 환경이 나쁘기 때문이다. 생산성에 대비해 상대적으로 높은 인건비, 다른 경쟁국에 비해 턱없이 비싼 땅값, 강성(强盛) 노조, 불편한 외국인 주거·교육 환경, 정부 규제 등에 대해 오래 전부터 여러 차례 지적이 있었지만 나아진 게 없다. 블룸버그 통신이 최근 성정한 '기업하기 좋은 나라 50개국' 순위에서 한국은 29위에 그쳐 홍콩의 1위를 위시한 다른 아시아 경쟁국들에 크게 뒤졌다.

(조선일보 사설 2012.04.02.)

＊ ＊ ＊

International companies are reluctant to make direct investments in Korea because of the unfavorable investment climate here.

For instance, the relatively high labor costs against productivity, the exorbitant land price as compared to the other competitive countries, the strong unions, the inconvenient housing conditions and unfavorable educational environment for the foreigners, plus the government regulations — these are some of the key issues, which, though often raised thus far, still remain to be resolved.

Recently, among the 50 countries picked by Bloomberg News as the favorable business environments Korea ranked 29th, lagging far behind the other competitive Asian countries, including Hong Kong, which was placed first.

 해설

1. 외국 기업이 국내 직접투자를 꺼리는 것은 우리나라의 투자 환경이 나쁘기 때문이다.

>>> International companies are reluctant to make direct investments in Korea because of the unfavorable investment climate here.

- **international/ global company:** 외국 기업
- **be reluctant to do:** ~하길 꺼린다 (= be unwilling/ indisposed/ hesitant to do)
- **make investments in:** ~에 투자하다 (= invest in)
- **unfavorable investment climate:** 좋지 않은 투자 환경 (= hostile investment environment)

2. 생산성에 대비해 상대적으로 높은 인건비, 다른 경쟁국에 비해 턱없이 비싼 땅값, 강성(强盛) 노조, 불편한 외국인 주거·교육 환경, 정부 규제 등에 대해 오래 전부터 여러 차례 지적이 있었지만 나아진 게 없다.

>>> (a) For instance, the relatively high labor costs against productivity, the exorbitant land price as compared to the other competitive countries, the strong unions, the inconvenient housing conditions and unfavorable educational environment for the foreigners, plus the government regulations — these are some of the key issues, which, though often raised thus far, still remain to be resolved.

• the relatively high labor costs against: ~에 대비해 상대적으로 높은 인건비

• against: ~에 대비해

• the exorbitant land price: 엄청난 땅값 (exorbitant = prohibitive; outrageous; steep)

• (as/ when) compared to/ with: ~과 비교해서 (= relative to)

• the strong unions: 강성 노조

• inconvenient/ poor housing condition: 불편한 주거 환경

• unfavorable educational environment: 좋지 않은 교육환경

• the government regulations: 정부 규제

>>> - these are some of the key issues, which, though often raised thus far, still remain to be resolved.

• raise issues: 문제를 제기하다 (= point out issues; bring up issues)

• thus far: 지금까지 (= up until now)

• resolve issues: 문제를 처리하다 (= address issues/ problems)

- **remain to be done**: 아직도 끝나지 않은 상태이다

- **remain to be resolved**: 아직도 해결돼야 하는 상태이다 (= remain to be adequately addressed)

>>> **(b) The persistent problems of the relatively high labor costs against productivity …. and the government regulations, although they have often been pointed out up until now, have yet to be resolved.**

- **the persistent problems of**: 고질적인 문제
- **have yet to be/ do**: 무언가가 아직 해결되지 못한 상태에서 ~돼야 할 일로 남아있다

3. 블룸버그 통신이 최근 성정한 '기업하기 좋은 나라 50개국' 순위에서 한국은 29위에 그쳐 홍콩의 1위를 위시한 다른 아시아 경쟁국들에 크게 뒤졌다.

>>> **Recently, among the 50 countries picked by Bloomberg News as the favorable business environments Korea ranked 29th, lagging far behind the other competitive Asian countries, including Hong Kong, which was placed first.**

- **pick A as B**: A를 B(의 자격으로) 선택하다 (= choose/ select A as B)
- **favorable business environment**: 기업하기 좋은 환경
- **(be) ranked 29th**: (어떤 순위에서) 29위를 차지하다 (= (be) placed as)
  cf **be rated at**: ~으로 평가되다
      be graded as: ~로 분류되다
- **lag/ fall behind something**: 무엇에 뒤떨어지다 (= trail something)
- **(be) placed first**: 1위를 차지하다 (= be ranked first)

1. 흡연 습관은 끊기가 힘들지만 불가능한 것은 아니다.

- 흡연 습관: a smoking habit

- 습관을 버리다: kick/ break the habit

- ~이 불가능하지는 않지만 ~하기가 힘들다: ~ is difficult, if not impossible, to do.

>>> **The smoking habit is difficult, if not impossible, to kick.**

2. 한국은 새로운 과학 기술 사용면에서 서양에 뒤질 수 없다.

- 새로운 과학 기술: new technology

- ~의 사용 면에서: in using ~

- 남에 뒤지다: fall/ lag behind others

- ~하는 것을 허용할 수 없다: cannot afford to do

  cf ~을 하지 않을 수 없다: cannot afford not to do

>>> **Korea cannot afford to fall behind the West in using new technology.**

13

늘어나는 커피 전문점

번역과 영작

   주변에 보면 하루가 다르게 늘어나는 게 커피전문점이다. 지난 해 말 전국에 있는 커피전문점은 1만 2381개로, 1년 새 54%가 늘었다. 말 그대로·우후죽순이다. 그런데도 목 좋은 곳이면 어디나 젊은이들로 북적인다. 3,000원짜리 라면으로 점심을 때워도 커피는 전문점에서 5,000원을 주고 마시는 게 요즘 젊은이들이다. 나도 가끔 가지만 원가에 비해 터무니없이 비싼 커피값을 생각하면 속이 쓰린다.

(중앙일보 2012.06.29.)

＊ ＊ ＊

   Looking around our surrounding areas, we can't help noticing that new coffee houses keep springing up every day.

   As of the end of last year, the total number of coffee houses in Korea jumped up to 12,381, up 54% from the year earlier. They are literally sprouting up all over the place.

Still, the coffee houses, especially those conveniently located, are thronged with today's young people, who don't mind paying 5,000 won for a cup of coffee in there, while they just gobble down 3,000 won ramen noodle for their lunch.

Occasionally, I also drop by a coffee house for a cup of coffee, but the very thought of having to pay for the coffee, which is unreasonably pricier than the cost price, rather leaves a sour taste in my mouth.

 해설

1. 주변에 보면 하루가 다르게 늘어나는 게 커피전문점이다.

>>> Looking around our surrounding areas, we can't help noticing that new coffee houses keep springing up every day.

- **look around**: 주변을 둘러보다
- **surrounding area**: 주변
- **can't help noticing/ seeing that**: ~인 것을 의식하지 않을 수 없다
  can't help doing that: ~하지 않을 수 없다 (= can't help but do)
  notice that: ~을 의식하다

- **coffee houses keep springing up:** 커피전문점이 매일 생기다 (= coffee houses proliferate)

- **keep doing:** 계속하다

- **spring up:** 무언가가 갑자기 생기다 (= pop up; sprout up; show up)
  - cf **Coffee houses are ubiquitous these days.** 요즘 커피 하우스는 여기저기 흔하게 퍼져있다.

2. 지난 해 말 전국에 있는 커피전문점은 1만 2381개로, 1년 새 54%가 늘었다. 말 그대로 우후죽순이다.

> >>> As of the end of last year, the total number of coffee houses in Korea jumped up to 12,381, up 54% from the year earlier. They are literally sprouting up all over the place.

- **as of the end of last year:** 지난해 말 현재 (= as from the end of last year)
  - **as of:** ~날 현재
  - **the end of:** ~의 끝

  It's the end of the line? (상점 등에서 줄 섰을 때) 여기가 줄 끝입니까?

- **jump to:** ~으로 늘어나다 (= rise/ grow to; increase)

- **, up 58%:** 58% 증가하다 (= by 58%)

- **from the year earlier:** 1년 전 (= from the past year; from the same period during the past year; year on year; from a year earlier; from the same time a year ago; from the previous year)

- **sprout up:** 우후죽순이다

3. 그런데도 목 좋은 곳이면 어디나 젊은이들로 북적인다. 3,000원짜리 라면으로 점심을 때워도 커피는 전문점에서 5,000원을 주고 마시는 게 요즘 젊은이들이다.

>>> Still, the coffee houses, especially those conveniently located, are thronged with today's young people, who are don't mind paying 5,000 won for a cup of coffee in there, while they just gobble down 3,000 won ramen noodle for their lunch.

- **still:** 그런데도 (= nonetheless)

- **those conveniently located:** 편리한 곳에 위치한 커피전문점

- **be thronged with:** ~로 북적이다 (= be crowded with; be packed with, fill up with)
  The coffee houses fill up with today's young people. 커피 집은 젊은이들로 꽉 찼다.
  cf be packed like sardines: 빽빽이 들어차다
  The subway is packed like sardines with commuters. 지하철은 출근객들로 꽉 채워졌다.

- **today's young people:** 오늘날의 젊은이들 (= young people of today)

- **don't mind paying:** ~을 기꺼이 지불하다
    - **don't mind doing:** ~을 기꺼이 하다 (= be willing to do)

- **, while they just gobble down ramen noodles:** 라면을 급히 먹으면서 (= shovel ramen into their mouth)
    - **gobble down:** 게걸스럽게 먹다 (= gulp; chow down)
    - **shove food into one's mouth:** 음식을 입에 퍼 넣다

4. 나도 가끔 가지만 원가에 비해 터무니없이 비싼 커피값을 생각하면 속이 쓰린다.

>>> Occasionally, I also drop by a coffee house for a cup of coffee, but the very thought of having to pay for the coffee, which is unreasonably pricier than the cost price, rather leaves a sour taste in my mouth.

- **occasionally:** 가끔 (= from time to time; every now and then; at times; once in a while)

- **drop by:** 잠시 들르다 (= stop by; drop into; swing by; visit)
  cf **nurse a cup of coffee:** (커피나 술을) 서서히 마시다

- **the (very) thought of doing:** ~한다는 생각(만 해도)

- **unreasonably pricier:** 터무니 없이 비싼

- **cost price:** 원가

- **leave a sour taste in one's mouth:** 뒷맛이 씁쓸하다

관련 유용 표현

1. 오늘날의 몇몇 젊은이들은 지나가는 사람들이 보는 앞에서 열정적으로 포옹하는 것을 개의 치 않는다.

- 오늘의 젊은이: today's young people

- 지나가는 사람들이 보는 앞에서: in full view of the passersby

- 열정적인 포옹을 하다: be locked in a passionate embrace (= hug each other tightly)

- ~하는 것에 개의치 않다: never hesitate to do

>>> Some of today's young people never hesitate to get locked in a passionate embrace in full view of the passersby.

2. 이 지역 상점에서 구입한 가정용품의 가격이 다른 상점들보다 훨씬 비싼 것을 알고 뒷맛이 씁쓸했다.

- 이 지역 상점: a local store
- 가정용품의 가격: the price they charged me for a household item; the price of a household item
- 다른 상점들보다 훨씬 비싸다: (the price) is much higher than at the other stores
- ~을 알고 뒷맛이 씁쓸하다: leave a bad taste in one's mouth

>>> The discovery that the price they charged me for a household item I got from a local store is much steeper than at the other stores has left a bad taste in my mouth.

14 한국의 싼 공공요금

우리들은 한국의 공공요금이 세계에서 가장 싸다는 사실을 모르고 산다. 전기와 물값은 너무나 싸 그야말로 물처럼 쓴다. 의당 그래야 한다고 믿는다. 지하철 요금이 도쿄와 뉴욕의 3분의 1, 택시비는 도쿄의 4분의 1 수준이다. 도쿄에서 약 20분 택시를 타면 대략 2만원 정도가 나오는데 한국에서는 5,000원이면 뒤집어 쓴다.

(중앙일보 2012.06.26.)

* * *

Koreans are living here in Korea, seemingly unaware that they actually pay the lowest utility bills on the planet.

Electricity and water is so cheap that they tend to use it like there is no tomorrow. But they still believe there is nothing wrong with that.

As for transportation costs, subway fares in Korea are a third of what they charge in Tokyo or in New York, while taxi fares are only a quarter of what you pay in Tokyo.

For instance, if you take a taxi in Tokyo, you will be charged about 20,000 won for a twenty-minute ride, whereas in Korea 5,000 won is more than enough for a ride of the same length of time.

 해설

1. 우리들은 한국의 공공요금이 세계에서 가장 싸다는 사실을 모르고 산다.

>>> (a) Koreans are living here in Korea, seemingly unaware that they actually pay the lowest utility bills on the planet.

- **be unaware that:** ~을 모르다 (= be oblivious to the fact that)
- **pay the lowest utility bills:** 가장 싼 공공요금을 납부하다 (= pay the utility bills at the lowest rate)
  pay the bills: 각종 공공요금을 지불하다　**cf** **foot the bill:** (많은 비용을) 부담하다
- **on the planet:** 지구상에서 (= on earth; in the whole world)

>>> (b) Koreans, living as they do in Korea, don't seem to realize that they pay the lowest utility bills in the whole world.

- **Koreans, living as they do in Korea, …:** 한국인은 한국에 살면서 ~ 하다

- realize that: ~을 깨닫다
- pay the lowest utility bills: 가장 싼 공공요금은 내다

2. 전기와 물값은 너무나 싸 그야말로 물처럼 쓴다. 의당 그래야 한다고 믿는다.

>>> Electricity and water is so cheap that they tend to use it like there is no tomorrow. But they still believe there is nothing wrong with that.

- so cheap that: 너무 싸기 때문에 ~하다
- use something like/ as if there is no tomorrow: 앞으로 어떻게 되든 상관 없다는 듯이 ~을 막 쓰다 (= use ~ to their heart's content; use ~ as much as they want; use ~ all they want; use ~ like water)
- there is nothing wrong with that: 아무 잘못이 없다

3. 지하철 요금이 도쿄와 뉴욕의 3분의 1, 택시는 도쿄의 4분의 1 수준이다.

>>> As for the transportation costs, subway fares in Korea are only a third of what they charge in Tokyo or in New York, while taxi fares are a quarter of what you pay in Tokyo.

- as for: ~에 관해서는
- a third of: ~의 3분의 1
- what is charged in Tokyo: 도쿄에서 요구하는 금액
- taxi fare: 택시 요금
- a quarter of: ~의 4분의 1

4. 도쿄에서 약 20분 택시를 타면 대략 2만원 정도가 나오는데, 한국에서는 5,000원이면 뒤집어 쓴다.

>>> For instance, if you take a taxicab in Tokyo, you will be charged about 20,000 won for a twenty-minute ride, whereas in Korea 5,000 won is more than enough for a ride of the same length of time.

- **take a taxicab/ taxi**: 택시를 타다
- **be charged 20,000 won for**: ~의 대가로 20,000원의 요금이 청구되다
- **be more than enough for**: ~하는데 충분하고도 남다
- **a ride of the same length of time**: 같은 시간 동안의 승차 (= a ride of the same amount of time)

C 관련 유용 표현

1. 아래 층에 사는 사람들이 소음 때문에 방해되지 않는 한 밤에 아파트에서 파티를 여는 것은 아무 문제가 되지 않는다.

- 아래 층에 사는 사람들: the people living on the floor below
  on the floor below: 아래 층
- ~때문에 방해되다: be disturbed by
- 파티를 열다: throw a party (= hold/ have/ give a party)
- ~을 하는 것이 아무 잘못이 없다: there is nothing wrong with doing

>>> There is nothing wrong with throwing a party in an apartment at night as long as the people living on the floor below are not disturbed by the noise from the house party.

2. 우리는 때때로 배우자의 희생을 당연시 하고 고맙다는 사실을 모르고 산다.

- 배우자의 희생을 당연시하다: take for granted the sacrifices our spouses make
- take something for granted: 무엇을 당연한 것으로 알다

   Don't take anything for granted. 무엇이고 당연시 하지 말라.
- 배우자에게 고맙다는 사실을 모르다: forget how grateful we are to our spouses
- 살다: go through our daily life

>>> As we go through our daily life, we often forget how grateful we are to our spouses, taking their great sacrifices for granted.

15

여성의 고용 부족

번역과 영작

　여직원의 임신과 출산을 비용만으로 보는 기업가들이 있다면 자본주의 진화를 위한 인식전환에 늦기 전에 동참해야 한다. 임신·출산·육아를 위해 보장된 휴가 사용마저 눈치를 봐야 한다면 성장과 복지의 선순환을 위한 어떠한 노력도 무용지물이 되어버릴 것이다. 기업들도 말로만 남녀평등을 생색낼 것이 아니라, 여성 인력의 고용 안정을 위하여 대체 인력 지원과 보장에도 정부와 발 맞추어 힘을 보태야 한다.

(조선일보 2012.03.28.)

* * *

　Should any of the entrepreneurs view the female employees' pregnancy and childbirth merely as the labor costs, they would do well to join others in changing their perception of the capitalistic evolution before it's too late.

As long as female workers do not even feel free to take time off for maternity leave, to which they are entitled, any attempts at the virtuous circle of economic growth and public welfare are ultimately bound to fail.

Therefore, instead of just paying lip service to the idea of equality between men and women, the private companies, by working closely with the government, should step up their effort to support and ensure the use of the alternative manpower in order to sustain the stable employment of the female workforce.

 해설

1. 여직원의 임신과 출산을 비용만으로 보는 기업인들이 있다면 자본주의적 진화를 위한 인식 전환에 늦기 전에 동참해야 한다,

>>> Should any of entrepreneurs view the female employees' pregnancy and childbirth merely as labor costs, they would do well to join others in changing their perception of capitalistic evolution before it's too late.

• Should any of the entrepreneurs view = If any of the entrepreneurs should view

- **view A as B:** A를 B로 간주하다 (= see/ regard/ perceive/ think of A as B)

- **labor costs:** 인건비

- **would do well to do:** ~하는 것이 좋다 (= would be better off doing; would be well advised to do; had better do)

- **join someone in doing:** 아무개와 함께 ~을 하다

- **change one's perception/ view of:** ~의 인식을 바꾸다

- **capitalistic evolution:** 자본주의적 진화

- **before it's too late:** 더 늦기 전에
  You had better take a quick action before it's too late. 더 늦기 전에 빨리 조치하는 것이 좋을 것이다.

2. 임신·출산·육아를 위해 보장된 휴가 사용 마저 눈치를 봐야 한다면, 성장과 복지의 선순환을 위한 어떠한 노력도 무용지물이 되어 버릴 것이다.

>>> As long as the female workers do not feel free to take time off for maternity leave, to which they are entitled, any attempts at the virtuous circle of economic growth and public welfare are ultimately bound to fail.

- **as long as:** ~을 하는 한

- **do not feel free to do:** ~을 자유롭게 하지 못하다 (= be cautious about doing; feel compelled to figure out what their bosses have in mind; try to get a sense of what their bosses think of)

- **take time off for maternity leave:** 출산 휴가를 받다
  - **take time off (work):** 잠시 (직장에서) 휴가를 얻다 (= take a leave from one's job)
  - **maternity leave:** 출산 휴가
    cf be on sick/ maternity leave: 병가/ 출산 휴가 중이다

- **be entitled to**: ~을 받을 권리가 있다
- **virtuous circle of**: ~의 선순환 **cf** **vicious circle of**: ~의 악순환
- **attempts at ~ are bound to fail**: 어떤 시도가 실패로 돌아가다
  - **be bound to do**: ~할 가능성이 크다 (= be likely to do)
  - **attempts fail**: 시도가 실패하다

3. 말로만 남녀의 평등을 생색 낼 것이 아니라, 여성 인력의 고용 안정을 위하여 대체 인력 활용을 위한 지원과 보장에도 정부와 발 맞추어 힘을 보태야 한다.

>>> Therefore, instead of paying lip service to the idea of equality between men and women, the private companies, by working closely with the government, should step up their effort to support and ensure the use of the alternative manpower in order to sustain the stable employment of the female workforce.

- **pay lip service to**: ~를 말만 앞세우다
  cf **practice what you preach**: 말을 행동으로 옮기다 (= walk the walk)
- **the idea of equality between A and B**: A와 B 사이의 평등 개념
- **work closely with**: ~와 긴밀히 협동하다 (= in coordination with)
- **step up one's effort to do**: ~을 하기 위해 더 노력하다 (= do more to do; go the extra mile to do)
- **the use of the alternative manpower**: 대체 인력 활용
- **sustain the stable employment of the female workforce/ labor force**: 여성 인력의 안정적 고용을 지속하다

1. 나는 내년에 하와이로 가족여행을 떠나기 위해 한 주 동안 일을 쉬기로 결정했다.

- ~로 가족여행을 떠나다: take a family vacation to; go on a family trip to
- 한 주 동안 일을 쉬다(직장에 안 나가다): take a week off

  cf take time off: (직장에서 시간을 내) 집에서 쉬다

- ~하기로 결정하다: decide to do

>>> I have decided to take a week off next year to take a family vacation to Hawaii.

2. 회사가 남녀 동등권을 말로만 내세우지 말고 행동으로 보여줘야 한다고 믿는다.

- 남녀 동등권: the idea of equality between men and women
- ~을 말로만 내세우다: pay only lip service to
- 행동으로 보여주다: practice what you preach; put one's money where one's mouth is

>>> We believe that, instead of paying only lip service to the idea of equality between men and women, the company should practice what it preaches.

cf Women often hit the glass ceiling in the workplace: 여성들은 흔히 직장에서 높은 자리에 올라가지 못하는 차별대우를 받는다.

The woman shattered the glass ceiling as the CEO of the company: 그 여성은 회사 사장으로 여성의 차별을 극복했다.

- glass ceiling: 여성 또는 특정 외국인이 직장에서 겪는 차별

한국의 경제 발전

번역과 영작

한국 사람은 모두 1등을 향해 달려가는 사람들만 있다고 해도 과언이 아니다. 전쟁 후 폐허가 된 땅에서 세계 최고의 물건을 만들지 않으면 팔리지 않는다는 일류 정신은 오늘날 한국이 경제 대국으로 성장한 원동력이 되기도 했다.

(중앙 San Francisco)

* * *

Perhaps it's no exaggeration to say that everyone in Korea is competing to take first place in a race.

In Korea, which has risen from the ashes following the Korean War, the best-pursuing spirit shown by the Korean people, who believe that anything made in the country is not marketable unless it is the best of its kind there is on the global markets, is deemed to be the driving force behind the Korea's rapid development into a great economic power today.

1. 한국 사람은 모두 1등을 향해 달려가는 사람들만 있다고 해도 과언이 아니다.

>>> Perhaps it's no exaggeration to say that everyone in Korea is competing to take first place in a race.

- **It's no exaggeration to say that:** ~라고 말해도 과언이 아니다 (= it's not an overstatement to say that; It's not a stretch to say that)
  cf **blow something out of proportion:** ~을 과장하다
  make a dream out of something: 사소한 일에 야단법석을 떨다
  make a mountain out of a molehill: 침소봉대하다
  I don't want to sound melodramatic: 내 말이 지나치게 과장되게 들리지 않았으면 좋겠다.
- **compete to do:** ~을 위해 경쟁하다 (= vie to do)
- **take first place:** 1등을 하다 (= finish first; come in first)
- **in a race:** 경주에서

2. 전쟁 후 폐허가 된 땅에서 세계 최고의 물건을 만들지 않으면 팔리지 않는다는 일류 정신은 오늘날 한국이 경제 대국으로 성장한 원동력이 되기도 했다.

>>> In Korea, which has risen from the ashes following the Korean War, the best-pursuing spirit shown by the Korean people, who believe that anything made in the country is not marketable unless it is the best of its kind there is on the global markets, is deemed to be the driving

force behind the Korea's rapid development into a great economic power today.

- **rise from the ashes**: 폐허에서 일어서다 (= rise from the ravages of (war))

- **following the Korean War**: 한국 전쟁 후

- **the best-pursuing spirit shown by the Korean people**: 한국인이 가진 '최고 추구'의 정신

  cf The spirit is willing but the flesh is weak. 마음이야 간절하지만 몸이 말을 듣지 않는다.

- **be marketable**: ~이 팔리다 (= be saleable)

- **be the best of its kind there is on the global markets**: 세계 시장에 있는 같은 종류 중 최고품

  - **be the best of its kind**: 같은 종류에서 최고품이다

  - **on the global markets**: 세계 시장에서

- **be deemed/ considered to be**: ~으로 간주 되다

- **the driving force behind Korea's rapid development**: 한국이 급성장한 원동력
  (= the driving force behind the rapidity with which the economic development has been made in Korea)

  - **the driving force**: 원동력

  - **behind something**: ~의 이면에

- **development into**: ~로의 발전

- **a great economic power**: 큰 경제력

1. 편안한 업무 환경이 산업 생산성을 크게 증가시킨다 해도 과언이 아니다.

- 편안한 업무 환경: a comfortable working environment
- 산업 생산성: industrial productivity
- ~을 증가시키다: lead to a (substantial) increase in; bring about an increase
- ~라 해도 과언이 아니다: It's no exaggeration to say that; It's not an overstatement to say that
- lead to/ increase productivity: 생산성을 증가시키다 (= boost productivity)

>>> **It's no exaggeration to say that a comfortable working environment will lead to substantial increase in industrial productivity.**

2. 한국이 경제 대국으로 성장한 원동력으로 한국인들의 과도한 교육열도 한몫 한다.

- 한국인들의 과도한 교육열: the boundless enthusiasm shown by Koreans for education; the insatiable desire Koreans have for education
- 한몫 하다: play a role in (= contribute to)

>>> **The boundless enthusiasm shown by Koreans for their children's education has played a role in the rapid development into a great economic power.**

Part 3

사회

17

행복의 조건

번역과 영작

진정한 행복이란 무엇이라고 생각하세요? 보통 아이가 공부를 잘하고 뛰어난 재능을 발휘하면 행복하리라 생각하나요? 하지만 남과의 비교나 경쟁을 행복의 기준으로 삼으면 그 기준에 도달하지 못할 때 삶 자체를 불행하다고 인식하게 되지요. 저는 행복에 대한 개념이 자신만을 위한 게 아니라 남과 더불어 살 때 느끼는 것으로 바뀌어야 한다고 생각합니다.

(월간 마음수련 2012.03.01.)

* * *

What do you think is true happiness?

Do you believe you would be happy if your kids were showing special talents as well as doing well in school?

However, if comparison with others or competitiveness is used as the sole criterion for measuring the level of happiness, life itself would be considered unhappy until that very criterion is fully satisfied.

Therefore, I, for one, take the view that the concept of happiness should be redefined as the kind of feeling that you get when you get along well with others instead of thinking only of yourself.

해설

1. 진정한 행복이란 무엇이라고 생각하세요? 보통 아이가 공부를 잘 하고 뛰어난 재능을 발휘하면 행복하리라 생각하나요?

> >>> What do you think is true happiness? Do you believe you would be happy if your kids were showing special talents as well as doing well in school?

- What do you think is true happiness? (= How do you define true happiness?; What is your definition of true happiness?; What do you think is the meaning of happiness?)
- show/ have talents: 특별한 재능을 발휘하다
    - special talents: 특별한 재능
- do well in school: 공부를 잘하다 (= be a good student)

2. 하지만 남과의 비교나 경쟁을 행복의 기준으로 삼으면 그 기준에 도달하지 못할 때 삶 자체를 불행하다고 인식하게 되지요.

>>> However, if comparison with others or competitiveness is used as the sole criterion for measuring the level of happiness, life itself would be considered unhappy until that very criterion is fully satisfied.

- **comparison with others**: 남과의 비교

  🟦 **stack up A against B**: A와 B를 비교하다

- **use A as the criterion for measuring B**: A를 가지고 B를 측정하는 기준으로 정하다

  (= use A as a benchmark against which to measure B; use A as standard by which to measure B)

- **satisfy/ meet the criterion**: 기준을 충족시키다

3. 저는 행복에 대한 개념이 자신만을 위한 게 아니라 남과 더불어 살 때 느끼는 것으로 바뀌어야 한다고 생각합니다.

>>> (a) Therefore, I, for one, take the view that the concept of happiness should be redefined as the kind of feeling that you get when you get along well with others instead of thinking only of yourself.

- **I, for one,**: 나 자신은 → 강조하는 뜻으로

- **take the view that**: ~의 견해를 취하다 (= my view is that; in my view; my take on that is that; for my money; in my opinion)

- **the concept of happiness**: 행복의 개념

- **redefine A as B**: A를 B라고 재정의하다

- the kind of feeling that you get when: ~할 때 느끼는 감정
- get/ have/ experience feeling: ~의 느낌을 갖다
- get along (well) with someone: 아무개와 잘 어울리다, 더불어 살다
- think only of yourself: 자신의 이익만을 생각하다 (= do something for one's own sake)

>>> (b) Therefore, for my part, I would broaden the definition of happiness to include the way you feel as you get along with others rather than doing anything for your own sake.

- for my part: 나로서는
- broaden the definition of A to include B: B가지 A의 정의에 포함시키다
- the way you feel as you get along with others: 다른 이들과 어울릴 때 느끼는 감정
- do anything for your own sake: 무엇이고 자신만을 위해서 하다

.

1. 행복은 단지 돈을 소유하는 데 있는 것이 아니다. 행복은 어떤 일을 이루는 기쁨과 창조적 노력의 설레는 마음 속에 있다.

- (행복은) ~에 있다: (happiness) lies in
- 돈의 소유: the possession of money
- 어떤 일을 이루는 기쁨: the joy of achievement
- 창조적 노력의 설렘: the thrill of creative effort

>>> Happiness lies not in the mere possession of money; it lies in the joy of achievement, in the thrill of creative effort.

(Theodore Roosevelt)

2. 요즘 대도시 젊은이들은 식당에서 혼자 밥을 먹는데 익숙하다. 남과 더불어 사는 즐거움에 관심을 두지 않는 것 같다.

- 요즘 대도시 젊은이들: the young people of today in big cities
- 혼자 밥을 먹는데 익숙하다: be used to eating all by oneself/ alone
- 남과 더불어 사는 즐거움: enjoying the company of other people; feeling the joy of getting along with other people; getting pleasure from getting along with other people
- 관심을 두지 않는 것 같다: don't seem to get interested in (= not get pleasure from/ don't care to do)

>>> The young people of today in big cities are used to eating in a restaurant all by themselves; they don't seem to get pleasure from getting along with other people.

18

40대 한국인의 수난

A

번역과 영작

한국의 40대를 규정하는 두 단어는 부담과 불안이다. 주택비 부담에 자녀 학비와 사교육비 부담에 허리가 휜다. 집값 폭락으로 가장 고통을 겪는 것도 40대다. 이들은 노후 준비도 변변히 해놓은 게 없는데 언제 퇴출될지 모른다는 불안감에 시달리고 있다. 1980년대에 대학을 다닌 40대는 신군부에 맞서 민주화를 이루어냈다는 자부심에 충만한 세대이기도 하다.

(중앙일보 2013.05.07.)

＊ ＊ ＊

Perhaps "burden" and "uneasy" are the two simple words which aptly describe the Korean men in their 40's, who are now struggling with the burden of paying their kids' school expenses, including private tuition fees, and meeting their mortgage payments.

Hit the hardest by the fallout from the collapse of the housing markets in

Korea, the people in this age group, who have barely enough money saved to retire, are now living in constant fear of losing their jobs.

Still these people, who went to college back in 1980's take great pride in their success in the fight for democratization in Korea against the neomilitary.

 해설

1. 한국의 40대를 규정하는 두 단어는 부담과 불안이다. 주택비 부담에 자녀 학비와 사교육비 부담에 허리가 휜다.

>>> (a) Perhaps "burden" and "uneasy" are the two simple words which aptly describe the Korean men in their 40's, who are now struggling with the burden of paying their kids' school expenses, including private tuition fees, and meeting their mortgage payments.

• **aptly describe the Korean men in their 40's**: 40대의 한국인을 적절히 말해주다

　• **the Korean men in their 40's**: 40대의 한국 남자

• **describe someone**: (사람의 모습, 행동을) 묘사하다 (= define/ sum up)

• **struggle with the burden of doing**: ~을 하는 부담에 허덕이다 (= shoulder the burden of doing)

　• **struggle with**: ~에 허리가 휘다, 허덕이다

• **pay the school expenses**: 학비를 대다

- school expenses including private tuition fees: 사교육비가 포함된 학비
- meet their home mortgage payments: 주택 융자금을 납부하다 (= pay mortgage)

>>> (b) The plight of the Koreans in their 40's, who are now burdened with their kids' school expenses including tuition fees and their mortgage payments, can be summed up just in two simple words "uneasy" and "burden."

- the plight of: ~의 곤경
- be burdened with: ~의 부담이 지워지다
- be summed up in: ~으로 압축해서 묘사하다

2. 집값 폭락으로 가장 고통을 겪는 것도 40대다. 이들은 노후 준비도 변변히 해놓은 게 없는데 언제 퇴출될지 모른다는 불안감에 시달리고 있다.

>>> (a) Hit the hardest by the fallout from the collapse of the housing markets in Korea, the people in this age group, who have barely enough money saved to retire, are now living in constant fear of losing their jobs.

- be hit the hardest by the fallout from the collapse of the housing market: 주택 가격 붕괴로 가장 심하게 타격을 받다
  - be hit hard by: ~의 큰 영향을 받다 (= be hard hit by; be severely affected by)
  - be fallout from: ~의 좋지 못한 결과
  - the collapse of the housing market: 주택 가격 붕괴
- the people in this age group/ bracket: 이 연령층의 사람들

- **have barely enough money saved to retire**: 은퇴 준비로 저축해 놓은 것이 별로 없다 (= have hardly any money set aside for their retirement; have yet to have their retirement plan put in place)

- **live in constant fear of losing jobs**: 일자리를 잃을까 봐 늘 두려워하면서 살다 (= live with the gloomy thought in the back of one's mind that his job is on the line; live, fearing that their jobs may be lost)

  - **live in fear of**: ~을 두려워하면서 살다

  - **lose a job**: 직업을 잃다 (= be laid off; get pink slip; get fired; get dismissed; get booted out; get axed; get fired; get sacked; get bumped)

    `cf` **keep a job**: 직업을 계속 유지하다

  - **with the thought that**: ~한 마음으로

  - **in the back of one's mind**: 마음 한 구석에

  - **one's job is on the line**: 직업이 위태롭다

>>> (b) Most severely affected by a dramatic plunge in the house prices in Korea, the people of this generation, with barely any money set aside for their retirement, are now living always concerned about dismissal from their current post.

- **be (severely) affected by**: ~에 (심하게) 영향을 받다

- **a (dramatic) plunge/ drop in the ~ price**: ~의 가격의 (급격한) 하락

- **the people of this generation**: 이 세대의 사람들

- **set aside money for**: ~을 위해 돈을 저축하다 (= save money for)

- **(feel) concerned about**: ~을 염려하다

- **dismissal from**: ~에서 면직되다

- **current post**: 현직

3. 1980년대에 대학을 다닌 40대는 신군부에 맞서 민주화를 이루어냈다는 자부심에 충만한 세대이기도 하다.

> >>> Still these people, who went to college back in 1980's take great pride in their success in the fight for democratization in Korea against the neomilitary.

- **take (great) pride in:** ~에 (큰) 자부심을 갖다
- **success in:** ~에서의 성공
- **the fight for democratization:** 민주화를 위한 투쟁
- **the fight against the neomilitary:** 신군부와의 싸움

관련 유용 표현

1. 어린 소녀가 자동차 사고로 그처럼 비극적으로 목숨을 잃는 모습을 보는 나의 마음은 이루 말로 표현할 수 없었다.

- 자동차 사고로: in a car crash
- 그처럼 비극적으로: so tragically
- 목숨을 잃는 모습을 보는 나의 마음: how I feel as I watch someone die
- 이루 말로 표현할 수 없다: words cannot describe (how I felt); I cannot find words to describe my feelings

>>> Words cannot describe how I felt as I was watching a little girl die so tragically in a car crash.

2. 은퇴 준비는 가급적 빨리 준비해야 하는데 그 중요성은 아무리 강조해도 지나지지 않다.

• 가급적 빠른 시일에: as soon as possible (= at one's earliest convenience)
• 은퇴 준비 시작의 중요성: the importance of starting to plan for one's retirement
• 아무리 강조해도 지나치지 않다: cannot be overemphasized

>>> The importance of starting to plan for your retirements cannot be overemphasized.

유치원 버스의 과속

19

번역과 영작

어린이들을 태운 통학용 승합차가 도로에서 위험하게 운행하는 경우가 적지 않다. 승차 정원을 초과하는 것은 물론이고 아이들을 태운 채 급격히 차로를 변경하거나 신호를 무시하는 등 교통법규를 위반하는 차량도 많다. 교통법규를 위반하다가 대형 차량과 충돌하면 승합차 안에 있는 아이들이 어떻게 될지 생각만 해도 끔찍하다. 한 어린이집 승합차에 탑승한 선생님이 차량이 정차한 곳에 아이를 내려놓고는 아이의 안전을 확인하지 않고 서둘러 출발하는 장면이 보였다.

(동아일보 2012.04.25.)

* * *

It's not uncommon for small school buses carrying small school children to run dangerously along the roads.

Many of the buses tend to break the traffic regulations by abruptly changing the lanes or by totally ignoring the traffic signals, not to mention the fact that in many cases they are overloaded with the children.

Therefore, I often shudder to think what could happen to the children if such a traffic violation should cause a head-on crash between the minibus and a large-sized vehicle.

Recently, a kindergarten teacher on the school bus was seen hurrying to leave immediately after dropping off kids at the bus stop without bothering to check to see if they are safe.

 해설

1. 어린이들을 태운 통학용 승합차가 도로에서 위험하게 운행하는 경우가 적지 않다.

>>> It's not uncommon for small school buses carrying small school children to run dangerously along the roads.

- **it's not uncommon for someone to do**: 아무개가 ~을 하는 것은 드물지 않다 (= it's common for someone to do; it's common practice for someone to do)
- **buses carrying children**: 어린이를 태운 버스 (= buses with children riding on them; buses filled with children)

  cf a plane with 100 passengers aboard/ on board: 승객 100명을 태운 비행기
- **buses run (along the roads)**: 버스가 (길을 따라) 운행하다

2. 승차 정원을 초과하는 것은 물론이고 아이들을 태운 채 급격히 차로를 변경하거나 신호를 무시하는 등 교통법규를 위반하는 차량도 많다.

>>> Many of the buses tend to break the traffic regulations by abruptly changing the lanes or by totally ignoring the traffic signals, not to mention the fact that in many cases they are overloaded with the children.

- **tend to do**: ~하는 경향이 있다 (= have a tendency to do)
- **break/ violate traffic regulations**: 교통 법규를 위반하다
- **by abruptly changing the lanes**: 급격히 차선을 변경함으로써 (= by weaving in and out of a lane; by swerving over both lanes of traffic)
  cf careen off: (사고 차가) 사고 직전에 노선을 넘나들다
- **by ignoring the traffic signals**: 신호를 무시하면서
- **not to mention (the fact that)**: (~라는 사실은) 말할 것도 없고
- **in many cases**: 많은 경우에
- **be overloaded with**: 사람을 너무 많이 태우다 (= exceed their seating capacity; load them over capacity)

3. 교통법규를 위반하다가 대형 차량과 충돌하면 승합차 안에 있는 아이들이 어떻게 될지 생각만 해도 끔찍하다.

>>> Therefore, I often shudder to think what could happen to the children if such a traffic violation should cause a head-on crash between the minibus and a large-sized vehicle.

- **shudder to think what could happen:** 어떻게 될지 생각하면 오싹 소름이 끼친다
  (= I shudder at the thought of what could happen; just thinking about what could happen makes me shudder; the very thought of what could happen makes me shudder)
- **a (head-on) crash/ collision between A and B:** A와 B의 (정면) 충돌

4. 한 어린이집 승합차에 탑승한 선생님이 차량이 정차한 곳에 아이를 내려놓고는 아이의 안전을 확인하지 않고 서둘러 출발하는 장면이 보였다.

>>> Recently, a kindergarten teacher on the school bus was seen hurrying to leave immediately after dropping off kids at the bus stop without bothering to check to see if they are safe.

- **be seen doing:** ~하는 것이 눈에 띄다
- **hurry to do:** ~을 서둘러 하다
- **immediately after doing:** ~을 하고 즉시
- **drop off someone:** 아무개를 차에서 내려주다 (= unload someone; let someone get out of (= off) a bus; let someone alight from a bus)
- **without doing:** ~을 하지 않고
  How can I complain without sounding petty? 어떻게 불평을 하면 쩨쩨하게 보이지 않습니까?
- **not bother to do:** ~을 하는 것에 신경을 쓰지 않다
- **check to see if someone is safe:** 아무개가 이상이 없는지 확인하다 (= check on someone)
    - **check to see if:** ~인지 확인하다
    - **someone is safe/ OK:** 아무개가 안전하다/ 이상이 없다

관련 유용 표현

1. 요즘 도로에서 운전 중 시비 끝에 아주 작은 일에도 참지 못하는 사람에게 폭행 당하는 일이 흔히 있다.

- 요즘: these days
- 도로에서 운전 중 시비: a road rage incident
- (화를 일으키는) 아주 작은 일에: at the slightest provocation (= over trivial matters)
- 화풀이를 하다: act out anger; unleash anger

  act out: (어떤 감정이나 생각을) 행동에 옮기다
- 폭행 당하다: get assaulted
- 흔히 있다: it's not uncommon for someone to do

>>> These days, it's not uncommon for some drivers to get assaulted in a road rage incident by some other drivers who would quickly act out anger at the slightest provocation.

2. 옛 고등학교 동문 중 한 명은 동창회에서 나를 본체 만체하고 떠났다.

- 옛 고등학교 동문 중 하나: one of my high school classmates
- 고등학교 동창회: high school class reunion
- 나를 본체 만체하다: without so much as acknowledging my presence

>>> One of my high school classmates left without so much as acknowledging my presence at the high school class reunion.

20

전력 대란

A

번역과 영작

올 여름 전력대란의 고비를 넘긴다 해도 자발적인 절전 호소만으로 구조적인 전력부족 사태를 극복할 수는 없다. 상대적으로 싼 전력요금이 전력수요 증가를 부추기고 있기 때문이다. 지난 겨울 10%의무 절전제를 시행했음에도 불구하고 실제 전력 소비는 전년보다 33%나 늘었다. 전력요금이 현실화 되지 않고는 전력수요를 줄이는 데 한계가 있다는 얘기다.

(중앙일보 2012.06.08.)

* * *

Although we can somehow manage to survive a severe energy crisis this summer, we cannot overcome the problem of the structural electricity shortage just by appealing for voluntary energy conservation, the reason being that the relatively low-electricity costs we now pay actually fuel the high demand for energy.

For instance, despite the mandatory reduction of 10% in electricity use, as implemented last winter, actual energy consumption has sharply increased by 33% from the previous year, which means there is a limit to what we can do to reduce the huge demand for energy use unless the current electricity rates get realistically readjusted.

 해설

1. 올 여름 전력대란의 고비를 넘긴다 해도 자발적인 절전 호소만으로 구조적인 전력부족 사태를 극복할 수는 없다. 상대적으로 싼 전력요금이 전력수요 증가를 부추기고 있기 때문이다.

>>> Although we can somehow manage to survive a severe energy crisis this summer, we cannot overcome the problem of the structural electricity shortage just by appealing for voluntary energy conservation, the reason being that the relatively low-electricity costs we now pay actually fuel the high demand for energy.

- **manage to do:** ~을 어렵사리 해내다
- **survive a crisis:** 위기를 견디다 (= handle/ manage/ avoid/ avert/ overcome a crisis)
- **overcome the problem of:** ~의 문제를 극복하다 (= resolve/ solve the problem of)
- **the structural electricity shortage:** 구조적인 전력 부족
- **by appealing for voluntary energy conservation:** 자발적인 절전을 호소하는 것만으로

- **the reason being that:** ~한 이유 때문에

- **pay the costs:** ~ 값을 치르다

- **fuel the high demand for:** ~의 수요를 부추기다 (= increase/ stimulate demand for)
  cf fuel speculation/ fears: 억측/ 공포를 부채질하다

2. 지난 겨울 10%의무 절전제를 시행했음에도 불구하고 실제 전력 소비는 전년보다 33%나 늘었다. 전력요금이 현실화 되지 않고는 전력수요를 줄이는 데 한계가 있다는 얘기다.

>>> For instance, despite the mandatory reduction of 10% in electricity use, as implemented last winter, actual energy consumption has sharply increased by 33% from the previous year, which means there is a limit to what we can do to reduce the huge demand for energy use unless the current electricity rates get realistically readjusted.

- **despite the mandatory reduction of 10% in electricity use, as implemented last winter:** 지난 겨울 시행한 의무적인 10% 절전에도 불구하고
  (= although we were requested to cut back on energy use by 10% under the government policy implemented last winter)

  - **mandatory reduction of 10% in:** ~에 대한 10%의 의무적 감축

  - **electricity use:** 전력 소비 (= electricity usage/ consumption)

  - **, as implemented last winter:** 지난 겨울 시행한

  - **implement reduction in electricity use:** 절전을 시행하다

  - **cut back on energy use:** 에너지를 절약하다 (= reduce/ curtail energy use)

  - **from the previous year:** 1년 전보다 (= from the year before; from the same time a year ago)

- **which means (that)** 그것은 ~을 뜻한다 (= , meaning that)

- **there is a limit to what we can do**: 우리가 할 수 있는 데는 한계가 있다 (= our ability to do ~ is limited)

- **reduce the demand for**: ~의 수요를 줄이다

- **unless the current electricity rates get realistically readjusted**: 현재의 전기 요금이 현실적으로 재조정되지 않으면 (= unless the current electricity rates are increased to the realistic level)

관련 유용 표현

1. 나는 영어 원어민과 영어 연습을 함으로써 나의 영어 실력, 특히 영어로 말하고자 할 때 나를 몹시 창피하게 했던 몇몇 단어 발음이, 좋아졌다고 당당하게 말할 수 있다.

- 원어민: native speakers (of English)
- ~와 영어연습을 함으로써: by practicing English on someone
- 영어 실력이 좋아지다: improve English
- 영어로 말하고자 할 때: as I tried to talk in English
- 나를 몹시 창피하게 하다: get me so embarrassed; cause me great embarrassment
- 영어 단어의 발음: the pronunciation of English words

>>> I must proudly say that I have substantially improved my English by practicing it on some native speakers, especially the pronunciation of certain English words, which often got me so embarrassed as I tried to talk in English.

2. 오늘날 우리에게 직면한 그 많은 사회문제를 해결하는 데는 한계가 있다.

- 우리에게 직면한 많은 사회문제: so many social problems facing us
- 문제를 해결하다: solve social problems; address/ handle/ deal with social problems
- ~을 하는 데는 한계가 있다: there is a limit to what we can do to do; our ability to do is limited

>>> There is a limit to what we can do to solve so many social problems facing us today.

21

교통 위반

번역과 영작

　얼마 전 밤늦게 한적한 서울 남산 도로를 지나다 빨간 신호등에 차를 세웠다. 자정 뉴스를 들으며 귀가하는 길이었는데, 뒤에서 빵빵거렸다. 차가 안 지나다니는데 왜 안 가냐는 것이었다. 그러더니 옆으로 차를 빼서 빨간 신호등을 무시하고 그냥 지나가버렸다. 이런 일이 이 날만 있었던 게 아니다. 새벽이든 밤이든, 대낮이든, 차가 없으면 빨간 신호등을 무시하고 지나가는 것을 어렵지 않게 목격할 수 있다. 과거엔 총알택시가 꼭두새벽이나 늦은 밤에 빨간 신호등을 무시하는 주범이었는데, 이제는 고급 승용차까지 아무렇지도 않게 빨간 신호등을 무시하고 지나간다.

(조선닷컴 2012.03.27.)

＊ ＊ ＊

　A short while ago, while driving along the quiet road on Mt. Namsan late at night, I stopped at a red light. I was on the way back home, listening to the midnight news on the radio, when all of a sudden I heard someone behind honking his horn.

He then grumbled that I had stopped there when there weren't any other cars there, and pulled out to get past my car, driving quickly through the red traffic light without stopping.

Actually, it wasn't the first time I witnessed what happened that night. Nowadays, it's not hard to find cars running a red light at dawn, at night or even in broad daylight, especially when there are no other cars around.

Unlike those days when the "bullet taxicabs" were the only kind of main offenders that ignored the traffic lights at dawn or late at night, these days even the luxury passenger cars are frequently spotted driving off in reckless disregard of a red light.

해설

1. 얼마 전 밤늦게 한적한 서울 남산 도로를 지나다 빨간 신호등에 차를 세웠다.

>>> A short while ago, while driving along the quiet road on Mt. Namsan late at night, I stopped at a red light.

• a short while ago: 얼마 전
• drive along the road: 그 길을 따라 운전하다

- **late at night**: 밤 늦게
- **stop at a red light**: 빨간 신호등에서 차를 세우다

2. 자정 뉴스를 들으며 귀가하는 길이었는데, 뒤에서 빵빵거렸다.

>>> I was on the way back home, listening to the midnight news on the radio, when all of a sudden I heard someone behind honking his horn.

- **I was on the way back home**: 집으로 가는 도중이다 (= I was heading back home; I was on my driving home)
- **listen to the midnight news on the radio**: 라디오에서 자정 뉴스를 듣다
- **all of a sudden**: 갑자기 (= suddenly)
- **someone behind**: 뒤에서 누군가
- **honk one's horn**: 빵빵거리다, 경적을 울리다 (= sound/ blown/ toot one's horn; beep at someone)

3. 차가 안 지나다니는데 왜 안 가냐는 것이었다. 그러더니 옆으로 차를 빼서 빨간 신호등을 무시하고 그냥 지나가버렸다.

>>> He then grumbled that I had stopped there when there weren't any other cars there, and pulled out to get past my car, driving quickly through the red traffic light without stopping.

- **when there weren't any other cars**: 아무 차도 없는데
- **pull out to get past my car**: 내 차 옆으로 빠져 지나가다 (= pull away from behind my car)

- **drive through a red traffic light**: 빨간 신호를 무시하고 지나가다 (= run a red light; drive through on a red light; violate a red light; jump a light; run the red)

4. 이런 일이 이 날만 있었던 게 아니다. 새벽이든 밤이든, 대낮이든, 차가 없으면 빨간 신호등을 무시하고 지나가는 것을 어렵지 않게 목격할 수 있다.

>>> Actually, it wasn't the first time I witnessed what happened that night. Nowadays, it's not hard to find cars running a red light at dawn, at night or even in broad daylight, especially when there are no other cars around.

- **it wasn't the first time that**: ~한 것은 그 때뿐이 아니다 (= this isn't the first time that)
- **witness**: (어떤 사건을) 목격하다
- **what happened that night**: 그날 밤 있었던 일
- **it's not hard to do**: ~하는 것은 어렵지 않다
- **find someone doing**: 아무개가 ~하는 것을 발견하다
- **run a (red) light**: 빨간 신호등을 무시하고 지나가다 (= drive through a red light)
  cf violate/ break/ flout traffic regulations
- **at dawn**: 새벽에 (= in the small/ early hours; in the wee hours)
- **in the broad daylight**: 대낮에
- **when there are no other cars around**: 다른 차들이 없으면/ 없는데

5. 과거엔 총알택시가 꼭두새벽이나 늦은 밤에 빨간 신호등을 무시하는 주범이었는데, 이제는 고급 승용차까지 아무렇지도 않게 빨간 신호등을 무시하고 지나간다.

>>> Unlike those days when the "bullet taxicabs" were the only kind of main offenders that ignored the traffic lights at dawn or late at night, these days even the luxury passenger cars are frequently spotted driving off in reckless disregard of a red light.

- **unlike those days when:** ~하던 과거와 달리

- **the only kind of main offenders that ignore the traffic lights:** 교통 신호를 위반하는 유일한 종류의 주범

    - **main offender:** 주범 (= speeder)

    - **ignore the traffic lights:** 교통 신호를 무시하다

- **luxury passenger cars:** 고급 승용차

- **spot someone doing:** 아무개가 ~하는 것이 눈에 띄다

- **drive off:** (차가) 가버리다

- **in reckless disregard of:** ~을 전혀 무시하며 (= in flagrant/ wanton/ blithe/ blatant disregard of)

 관련 유용 표현

1. 내가 영어로 외국손님을 대할 수 없기 때문에 그 자리의 후보자 명단에서 제외된 것을 알고 굴욕감을 느낀 것은 이번이 처음이 아니다

- **~을 잘하다:** be good at doing
- **외국 손님을 대하다:** handle the foreign customers (= deal with/ meet with/ visit with the foreign customers)

• ~을 알고 굴욕감을 느끼다: feel insulted/ mortified to learn that

• 이번이 처음이 아니다: it's not the first time that

>>> It's not the first time that I felt insulted to learn that I was excluded from the list of the candidates for the job just because I'm not good at handling the foreign customers in English.

2. 어떤 운전자들은 도로 1차로에서 추월하면서 규정속도를 무시해도 된다고 생각하는데 이는 잘못된 것이다.

• 어떤 운전자들: some drivers

• 1차로에서: on the fast lane

• 추월하다: pass other vehicles

• 규정속도를 무시하다: exceed/ violate the speed limit

• ~을 해도 된다고/ 괜찮다고 (생각하다): (think/ believe) it's OK to do; it's perfectly all right to do

>>> (a) Some drivers are wrong to believe that they can exceed the speed limit by passing other vehicles on the fast lane.

(b) Some drivers think it's perfectly all right to violate the speed limit by passing other cars along the fast lane, but they are simply wrong.

22

고령화 사회

번역과 영작

　최근 들어 그 어느 때보다 많은 숫자의 베이비부머들의 은퇴시기가 시작되었지만 지금 은퇴한다고 인생이 끝나는 것이 아니라 사실은 지금부터가 제2인생의 시작이다. 인구 고령의 사회가 현실로 다가오면서 앞으로는 100세까지 사는 것이 어려운 일이 아니다. 30~40년의 긴 노년을 어떻게 살아가야 할 것인지를 준비하는 것이 이제 큰 과제가 되었다. 예전 어르신들은 손주를 보면 자신이 늙었다는 생각을 하였지만 요즘은 증손주를 본 할머니, 할아버지인데 손수 운전하고 다니시는 분들이 주위에 적지 않게 계신다.

(여성중앙 2011.07.27.)

＊ ＊ ＊

　Now more than ever, a greater number of the baby boomers are starting to retire from their work. Retirement, however, is not the end of the world for them because it actually marks the beginning of the second phase of their life.

With an aging society fast becoming a reality in Korea, it's not unreasonable to expect people in the future to live to the age of 100.

Therefore, coming up with a plan to figure out how to fill a long period of 30 to 40 years in later life is everyone's responsibility.

Nowadays, it's not uncommon for great-grandmothers and great-grandfathers, in spite of their age, to drive around in their cars unlike in the old days when the elderly really felt their age as they watched their grandchildren.

 해설

1. 최근 들어 그 어느 때보다 많은 숫자의 베이비부머들의 은퇴시기가 시작되었지만 지금 은퇴한다고 인생이 끝나는 것이 아니라 사실은 지금부터가 제2의 인생의 시작이다.

>>> Now more than ever, a greater number of the baby boomers are starting to retire from their work. Retirement, however, is not the end of the world for them because it actually marks the beginning of the second phase of their life.

• **now more than ever**: 그 어느 때보다도 지금 (= like never before)

• **retirement is not the end of the world**: 은퇴가 인생의 끝이 아니다 (= doesn't mean the end of the world is looming/ the sky is falling)

• it marks the beginning of the second phase of their life: 그것은 제2의 인생의
시작이다 (= it marks a new stage in their life)

> • mark the beginning: ~의 시작이다 **cf** mark the end: ~의 마지막이다
> **cf** The ceremony marks the 60th anniversary of the end of the
> Second World War: 그 기념식은 세계제2차대전 종전 60주년을 기념한다.
>
> • the second phase/ stage of their life: 그들의 제2의 인생

2. 인구 고령의 사회가 현실로 다가오면서 앞으로는 100세까지 사는 것이 어려운 일이 아니다.

>>> With an aging society fast becoming a reality in Korea, it's not
unreasonable to expect people in the future to live to the age of 100.

• with something becoming a reality: ~가 현실화 되면서

> • an aging society: 고령화 사회
>
> • become a reality: 현실이 되다

• it's not unreasonable to do: ~하는 것은 무리가 아니다 (= It's common practice to do)

• expect A to do B: A가 B할 것으로 기대하다

• live up to the age of 100: 백세까지 살다 (= live to be 100)

3. 30~40년의 긴 노년을 어떻게 살아가야 할 것인지를 준비하는 것이 이제 큰 과제가 되었다.

>>> Therefore, coming up with a plan to figure out how to fill a long
period of 30 to 40 years in later life is everyone's responsibility.

• come up with a plan: 계획을 세우다
cf I can't come up with that kind of money: 나는 그렇게 많은 돈을 마련할 수 없다.

• a plan to figure out how to spend: 어떻게 보낼 것인가를 강구하는 계획

- a plan to do: ~할 계획

  - figure out how to do: ~하는 방법을 강구하다

- fill a period of 30-to-40 years: 30~40년의 긴 기간을 (~을 하면서) 보내다 (= spend 30-to-40 long years)

- be someone's responsibility: ~은 아무개가 할 일이다

- in later life/ years: 만년에

- be one's responsibility: ~가 해야 할 일이다

4. 예전 어르신들은 손주를 보면 자신이 늙었다는 생각을 하였지만 요즘은 증손주를 본 할머니, 할아버지인데 손수 운전해 다니시는 분들이 주위에 적지 않게 계신다.

>>> Nowadays, it's not uncommon for great-grandmothers and great-grandfathers, in spite of their age, to drive around in their cars unlike in the old days when the elderly really felt their age as they watched their grandchildren.

- it's not uncommon/ unusual for someone to do: 아무개가 ~을 하는 것은 드문 일이 아니다 (= it's common practice for someone to do)

- in spite of their age: 그 분들의 연세에도 불구하고 (= defying their age; despite age)

- drive around: 차를 몰고 다니다

- in their cars: 자신들의 차를 몰고

- unlike (in) the old days when: ~하던 옛날과 달리

- the elderly really felt their age: 연로하신 분들이 나이를 실감했다 (= the elderly suddenly felt old age creeping up on them)

  - feel one's age: 나이를 실감하다

- as they watched their grandchildren: 손주를 보면서 (= looking at their grandchildren; while watching their grandchildren)

1. 오늘날 사업을 시작하는 여성의 수가 현저히 늘면서 그들이 한국에서 가장 성공적인 회사를 운영하는 것은 흔히 있는 일이다.

- 사업을 시작하다: go into business; set up in business
- 여성의 수가 현저히 늘면서: with a significant increase in the number of women
- 회사를 운영하다: run a company
- A가 B를 하는 것은 흔히 있는 일이다: it is not uncommon for A to do B

>>> Today with a significant increase in the number of women going into business, it is not uncommon for them to run some of the most successful companies in Korea.

2. 취업난으로 인해 젊은이들은 대학 1학년부터 어떻게 취업준비를 할 것인가 강구해야 하는 판국이다.

- 취업난으로: facing difficulty in landing jobs/ seeking employment
- 젊은이들: the college students
- 1학년부터: from their freshman year on
- 어떻게 취업준비를 할 것인가: how to prepare for the jobs
- 강구해야 하는 판국이다: be put in a situation where they have to start figuring out

>>> Facing difficulty in landing jobs, the college students in Korea are put in a situation where they, from their freshman year on, have to start figuring out how to prepare for their employment.

㉓ 연금 사기

A 번역과 영작

일본에서는 2010년 가족들이 연금을 타기 위해 수십 년 전에 죽은 백골 상태의 부모 시신을 집안에 감추고 있다가 적발되는 사건이 잇따라 충격을 줬다. 당시 일본 정부는 연금 부정 수령을 막기 위해 전국적으로 고령자 생존 여부 확인작업을 벌여 가족들이 사망한 부모의 연금을 수령한 사례를 수백 건 적발했다.

(조선닷컴 2012.04.04.)

＊ ＊ ＊

In 2010 the Japanese people were stunned to find that a series of pension frauds were committed by some Japanese families, who, in order to continue to draw their late parents' pension, had been hiding in their homes the remains of their parents, who died scores of years earlier.

In an attempt to curb the fraudulent claims for the pension benefits, the Japanese government then engaged in checking nationwide to see if the elderly were still alive, when it discovered hundreds of cases where the Japanese family members knowingly kept collecting their deceased parents' pension.

B 해설

1. 일본에서는 2010년 가족들이 연금을 타기 위해 수십 년 전에 죽은 백골 상태의 부모 시신을 집안에 감추고 있다가 적발되는 사건이 잇따라 충격을 줬다.

>>> In 2010 the Japanese people were stunned to find that a series of pension frauds were committed by some Japanese families, who, in order to continue to draw their late parents' pension, had been hiding in their homes the remains of their parents, who died scores of years earlier.

• **be stunned to find that**: ~뜻밖에 ~을 알게 되어 몹시 놀라다 (= be shocked to learn that; be nonplused at; be dumbfounded by; be flabbergasted)

• **a series of**: ~의 연속, 일련의

• **pension frauds**: 연금 사기

• **commit frauds**: 사기를 치다

　cf 사기를 당하다: be conned; be taken for a ride; be swindled; be cheated

- draw/ collect one's pension: ~의 연금을 타다
- their late/ deceased parents: 고인이 된 부모
- (skeletal) remains: 유해
- scores of: 수십의

2. 당시 일본 정부는 연금 부정 수령을 막기 위해 전국적으로 고령자 생존 여부 확인작업을 벌여 가족들이 사망한 부모의 연금을 수령한 사례를 수백 건 적발했다.

>>> (a) In an attempt to curb the fraudulent claims for the pension benefits, the Japanese government then engaged in checking nationwide to see if the elderly were still alive, when it discovered hundreds of cases where the Japanese family members knowingly kept collecting their deceased parents' pension.

- in an attempt to do: ~을 할 시도로 (= as an effort to do; as a way of doing; in a bid to do)
- curb: ~을 억제하다 (= control)
- fraudulent claims for pension benefits: 부정 연금 수령 청구
- claim for: ~의 요구로 (= make/ file a claim for)
  The family of the victim made a claim for compensation. 그 희생자 가족은 보상을 요구했다.
- engage in: ~에 종사하다
- nationwide: 전국적으로 (= across the nation; throughout the nation)
- check to see if the elderly are still alive: 노인들이 아직 생존하는지 확인하다 (= to confirm/ verify the existence of the elderly)
  - check to see if: ~인지 알아보다

- **hundreds of:** 수백의

- **a case where:** ~한 사례 (= a case in which)

- **knowingly:** (불법인 줄) 알면서 (= wittingly)

- **collect pension:** 연금을 수령하다 (= draw/ get/ receive pension)

>>> (b) Then, the Japanese government, while going through the process of verifying nationwide the elderly's actual existence to prevent the fraudulent claims for pension, uncovered hundreds of cases of the Japanese families knowingly collecting their late parents' pension.

- **go through the process of doing:** ~을 하는 과정에서

- **verify the elderly's actual existence:** 고령자들의 실제 생존을 확인하다 (= confirm the identity of the elderly)

- **case of:** ~의 사례

 관련 유용 표현

1. 학창 시절에는 학업이 뒤졌지만 장차 그들이 선택한 직업에서 크게 성공한 사람들의 사례는 많다.

- 학창 시절에: in school
- 학업이 뒤지다: do poorly in school; lag behind the other students
- 그들이 선택한 직업에서: in their chosen careers

• 크게 성공하다: prove oneself to be successful

>>> **There are many cases in which those who were doing poorly in school have later proved themselves to be very successful in their chosen careers.**

2. 고등학교에서 남성 교사들의 여학생 성추행을 감추고 있다가 적발되는 사건이 잇따라 충격을 주고 있다.

• 고등학교에서: in high schools
• 남성교사들: male high school teachers
• ~의 사건이 잇달아: continual cases of
• 성추행하다: commit indecent act; commit sexual misconduct
• 적발되다: be accused of
• 감추고 있다가: secretly; without one's knowledge
• 충격을 주고 있다: be shocked to learn about

>>> **We are shocked to learn about continual cases of sexual misconduct by some male high school teachers, who stand accused of secretly committing indecent acts on female students in high schools.**

24

국수주의

번역과 영작

외국인 혐오를 부추기는 편협한 국수주의는 추방돼야 마땅하다. 이런 인종 차별 행위는 대한민국 공동체의 화합을 해치는 것은 물론 대외 이미지에도 악영향을 끼치기 때문이다. 포용과 화합을 중시하는 우리 전통에 어긋날뿐더러 반인권적이기도 하다. 대부분의 국내 거주 외국인은 사실 한국 사회의 필요에 의해 입국했다. 농촌 총각 문제를 해결하기 위해 외국인 신부와의 결혼을 주선했으며, 3D업종과 중소기업의 일손 부족을 메우기 위해 외국인 노동자들을 초청했다.

(중앙일보 2012.07.13.)

* * *

Curbing nationalism, which fans the flames of racial hatred in Korea, is the perfectly right thing to do.

Such racist attitude not only harms the social harmony in Korean society but also tarnishes the image of Korea abroad. Furthermore, it constitutes a gross violation of human rights, as well as going against the time-honored tradition of promoting inclusiveness and harmony in Korea.

After all, most foreign residents are here to fill the needs of the Korean people.

In fact, it was specially arranged for single Korean farm workers to find their partners from the other countries and for foreign labor to be here to do the difficult, dirty and dangerous work and to ease a shortage of a labor force faced by the small and medium-sized manufactures in Korea.

해설

1. 외국인 혐오를 부추기는 편협한 국수주의는 추방돼야 마땅하다.

>>> (a) Curbing nationalism, which fans the flames of racial hatred in Korea, is the perfectly right thing to do.

• curb nationalism: 국수주의의 확대를 막다 (= stun the growth of nationalism; end nationalism; stem the tide of nationalism; eradicate nationalism; stamp out nationalism; deter nationalism)

- **narrow-minded nationalism**: 편협한 국수주의 (= jingoism)

- **fan the flame of racial hatred**: 외국인 혐오를 조장하다 (= stir up/ incite racial hatred)

  - **racial hatred**: 외국인 혐오 (= racist behavior; racist bias)

- **be perfectly right thing to do**: 마땅히 해야 할 일이다 (= be fully justified)

>>> (b) It makes perfect sense to eradicate narrow-minded nationalism.

- **make sense to do**: ~하는 것은 타당하다, 도리에 맞다

- **eradicate nationalism**: 국수주의를 제거하다 (= root out/ stamp out nationalism)

2. 이런 인종 차별 행위는 대한민국 공동체의 화합을 해치는 것은 물론 대외 이미지에도 악영향을 끼치기 때문이다. 포용과 화합을 중시하는 우리 전통에 어긋날뿐더러 반인권 적이기도 하다.

>>> Such racist attitude not only harms the social harmony in Korean society but also tarnishes the image of Korea abroad. Furthermore, it constitutes a gross violation of human rights, as well as going against the time-honored tradition of promoting inclusiveness and harmony in Korea.

- **racist attitude**: 인종 차별 행위 (= racist bias)

- **harm the social harmony**: 사회의 화합을 해치다

- **tarnish the image of**: ~의 이미지를 손상시키다, 더럽히다

- **constitute a violation of human rights**: 인권 유린을 범하다

  - **constitute**: ~하는 행위가 되다

  Failure to complete the work by next week would constitute a breach of the contract. 내주까지 공사가 끝나지 않으면 계약 위반이 된다.

- violate human rights: 인권을 유린하다
- go against the time-honored tradition of: ~의 오랜 전통과 어긋나다 (= break with the long tradition of; fly in the face of the long tradition of)
- promote harmony: 화합을 촉진하다 (= embrace/ advocate harmony)

3. 대부분의 국내 거주 외국인은 사실 한국 사회의 필요에 의해 입국했다.

>>> After all, most foreign residents are here to fill the needs of the Korean people.

- after all: 어쨌든
- foreign residents: 외국인 거주민
- be here to do: ~하기 위해서 여기 있다, 살다
- fill the needs of: ~의 필요성을 충족시키다 (= meet/ satisfy/ serve the needs of)

4. 농촌 총각 문제를 해결하기 위해 외국인 신부와의 결혼을 주선했으며, 3D업종과 중소기업의 일손 부족을 메우기 위해 외국인 노동자들을 초청했다.

>>> In fact, it was formally arranged that single Korean farm workers would find their partners from the other countries and that foreign labor would be brought in here to do the difficult, dirty and dangerous work and to ease a shortage of a labor force faced by the small and medium-sized manufactures in Korea.

- it is arranged for A to B: A가 B를 하도록 주선하다
- find/ meet their partners from the other countries: 외국인 결혼 상대를 만나다

- alleviate/ ease/ address a shortage of the workforce: 노동력 부족을 메우다

    - ease: ~의 문제를 완화하다

- face/ experience a shortage of: ~의 부족을 겪다

    - a shortage of: ~의 부족

- workforce: 노동력

- small-and-medium sized manufacturers: 중소기업 규모의 제조업체

 관련 유용 표현

1. 내가 임신한 동안 집안 일을 돕기 위해 한국에서 어머니께서 와계시다.

- 한국에서 오신 어머님: my mom from Korea
- 임신 기간: during my pregnancy
- 집안 일을 돕다: help me with the daily chores
- ~하기 위해 여기 있다: be here to do

>>> My mom from Korea is here to help me with the daily chores during my pregnancy.

2. 결혼 전에 신랑과 신부가 호화혼수 때문에 불화가 생기는 일은 한국의 혼례 전통이 아니라고 생각한다.

- 호화혼수: expensive marriage gifts

- 주고 받음: exchange of

- 결혼 전에: prior to a marriage ceremony

- 불화가 생기다: have a bitter argument over/ about (= argue over; squabble over)

- 한국의 혼례 전통: the traditional/ established marriage custom in Korea

>>> I don't think it's traditionally acceptable for the bride and groom in Korea to get into a bitter argument over the exchanges of expensive wedding gifts prior to a marriage ceremony.

25

아기의 복권 당첨

A

번역과 영작

  뉴욕데일리 뉴스에 따르면 뉴욕에 살고 있는 파키스탄 출신 이민 여성이 2살된 딸과 함께 브룩클린 근처의 한 마켓에서 쇼핑을 하고 있었다. 그러다 계산 도중 딸이 갑자기 스크래치식 즉석 복권을 손에 쥐었다. 엄마가 복권을 다시 점원에게 돌려주려 했지만 그 아기는 떼를 쓰며 좀처럼 물러나지 않았다. 그 여성은 하는 수 없이 복권을 샀다. 그런데 그 복권이 이들에게 엄청난 행운을 안겨다 줬다. 100만 달러 당첨이었다. 2031년까지 세금을 제하고 매년 3만 1152달러를 받게 된 것이다.

(중앙일보 2012.03.16.)

* * *

  According to a *New York Daily* report, a female Pakistan immigrant living in New York City was doing the shopping with her two-year-old daughter at a store located in a Brooklyn area in N.Y.

What happened then was that, as she was paying for her purchases, her daughter quickly grabbed one of the instant scratch-off lottery tickets from the store.

And so the woman hurriedly tried to take it away from the baby to give it back to the store clerk but all to no avail. The baby wouldn't let go of it.

The woman therefore reluctantly bought the ticket, which unexpectedly turned out to be the one-million-dollar jackpot bringing great happiness to them.

She is now entitled to receive $31,152 after tax every year until 2031.

 B 해설

1. 뉴욕데일리 뉴스에 따르면 뉴욕에 살고 있는 파키스탄 출신 이민 여성이 2살된 딸과 함께 브룩클린 근처의 한 마켓에서 쇼핑을 하고 있었다.

>>> According to a *New York Daily* report, a female Pakistan immigrant living in New York City was doing the shopping with her two-year-old daughter at a store located in a Brooklyn area in N. Y.

• according to a *New York Daily* report: 뉴욕데일리 뉴스에 의하면 (= a *New York Daily* report publishes/ carries)

- *New York Daily*: 뉴욕데일리 신문

- according to: ~에 의하면

- newspaper reports: 신문은 ~을 보도하다 (= newspaper publishes/ carries/ prints)

- do the shopping: 쇼핑하다 (= go shopping)
  - cf shop around for: (가격, 품질을 비교하며) 쇼핑을 다니다
  - do groceries: 식료품을 구매하다, 장 보다

2. 그러다 계산 도중 딸이 갑자기 스크래치식 즉석 복권을 손에 쥐었다.

>>> What happened then was that, as she was paying for her purchases, her daughter quickly grabbed one of the instant scratch-off lottery tickets from the store.

- what happened then was that: 그 때 무슨 일이 있었느냐 하면 ~한 일이 생기다

- as she was paying for her purchases: 그 여성이 물건 값을 지불할 때

  - pay for: 지불하다

  - her purchases: 그녀가 구매한 물품

- grabbed one of the instant scratch-off lottery tickets from the store: 상점에서 즉석 복권을 집어 손에 쥐었다

  - grab A from B: B에서 A를 손으로 집다

  - an instant scratch-off lottery tickets: 스크레치식 즉석 복권

3. 엄마가 복권을 다시 점원에게 돌려주려 했지만 그 아기는 떼를 쓰며 좀처럼 물러나지 않았다.

>>> And so the woman hurriedly tried to take it away from the baby to give it back to the sales assistant but all to no avail. The baby wouldn't let go of it.

- **take A from B:** B로부터 A를 빼앗다

- **give A back to B:** B에게 A를 돌려주다

- **store clerk:** 점원 (= sales assistant)

- **all to no avail:** 소용이 없다 (= all of no avail; without success)

- **would not do:** 아무리 해도 ~을 하려고 하지 않다 (= stubbornly/ steadfastly/ adamantly/ obstinately/ persistently refused to do/ resistant to doing)

- **let go of something:** 뭔가를 (손으로 잡고 있다) 놓다 (= let something go; release something)

4. 그 부인은 하는 수 없이 복권을 샀다. 그런데 그 복권이 이들에게 엄청난 행운을 안겨다 줬다. 100만 달러 당첨이었다.

>>> The woman therefore reluctantly bought the ticket, which unexpectedly turned out to be the one-million-dollar jackpot bringing great happiness to them.

- **reluctantly bought the ticket:** 마지못해 그 복권을 샀다 (= unwillingly bought the ticket)

- **turn out to be:** ~이 되다, ~임이 판명되다 (= prove to be)

- **the one-million-dollar jackpot:** 당첨 복권 (= winning ticket/ the lottery for one million dollar) **cf** hit/ win a lottery: 복권에 당첨되다

- **bringing great happiness to:** ~에게 큰 행복감을 가져오다

5. 2031년까지 세금을 제하고 매년 3만 1152달러를 받게 된 것이다.

>>> She is now entitled to receive $31,152 after tax every year until 2031.

- be entitled to do: ~할 권리가 있다/ ~을 받을 권리가 있다

- after tax: 세금을 제하고 before tax 세전 ~plus tax: ~에 세금이 붙다

관련 유용 표현 {C}

1. 어린이 한 명이 공원 놀이터에서 실종되었다는 신고를 받고 경찰이 급파되었으나 그 어린이는 몇 마일 떨어진 숲 속에 누워있는 시신으로 발견되고 말았다.

- 공원 놀이터: the playground in a park
- 어린이가 ~에서 실종되었다고 신고되다: a child was reported missing from
- 경찰을 그곳으로 급파하다: dispatch police to
- 그곳에서 몇 마일 떨어진 숲 속에서: in the woods a few miles away
- ~을 하였지만 결과는 … 하였다(본래의 뜻이 이루어지지 않았다): ~only to find

>>> When a child was reported missing from the playground in a park, police were dispatched to the scene only to find his dead body lying in the woods a few miles away.

2. 나는 65세부터 사망 시까지 매달 세금을 제하고 1,000달러씩 받는 연금을 준비해 놓았다.

- 65세부터 사망 시까지: starting at 65 till my death
- 세금을 제하고: after tax
- 매달 1,000달러씩: $1,000 per month
- 받는 연금을 준비해놓았다: have a retirement plan put in place; have a retirement plan ready

• ~을 하기 위한 퇴직 연금 제도: a retirement plan to do

>>> I have a retirement plan put in place to collect $1,000 per month after tax starting at 65 till my death.

26
사회 발전의 조건

번역과 영작

사회가 지속 발전하기 위해서는 젊은 세대에게 꿈과 희망을 주어야 하며, 기회가 공정하게 열려 있어야 한다. 진정한 경쟁사회가 되어야 하는 것이다. 연줄이나 관계가 아닌, 실력으로 경쟁하는 사회가 되어야 한다. 부모를 잘 만나는 것이 성공의 결정적 요인이 되어서는 안 되는 것이다. 그러나 지금 우리 사회 구석구석의 모습은 우리 사회가 진정한 경쟁사회가 아님을 보여준다.

(중앙일보 2012.10.20.)

＊ ＊ ＊

In order to ensure sustainable social development in Korea the young generation must have a hope and dream with equal opportunities open to them.

It is also essential that Korea is a fairly competitive society, where, instead of family connection and relationships being used to advantage, young people are given a fair chance to pit their ability against each other without any privileged family background being a deciding factor in success.

However, from what we see happening across Korea now, Korea still has a long way to go before it can be called a truly competitive society.

 B 해설

1. 사회가 지속 발전하기 위해서는 젊은 세대에게 꿈과 희망을 주어야 하며, 기회가 공정하게 열려 있어야 한다.

   >>> In order to ensure sustainable social development in Korea the young generation must have a hope and dream with equal opportunities open to them.

   • in order to do: ~을 하기 위해서는
   • have a hope and dream: 꿈과 희망을 갖다
   • an opportunity is open to: ~에게 희망이 열려있다

2. 진정한 경쟁사회가 되어야 하는 것이다. 연줄이나 관계가 아닌, 실력으로 경쟁하는 사회가 되어야 한다. 부모를 잘 만나는 것이 성공의 결정적 요인이 되어서는 안 되는 것이다.

>>> It is also essential that Korea is a fairly competitive society, where, instead of family connection and relationships being used to advantage, young people are given a fair chance to pit their ability against each other without any privileged family background being a deciding factor in success.

- it is essential that: ~하는 것이 극히 중요하다

- instead of ~: ~ 대신 (= in lieu of~)

- family connection/ ties: 가족 간의 연줄

- a competitive society: 경쟁 사회

- use/ turn something to good advantage: 무엇을 유리하게 이용하다

  - use something to one's advantage: 무엇을 ~에게 유리하게 이용하다 (= use something to achieve/ reach/ attain one's goal)

- give a fair chance to pit one's ability against each other: 남과 실력을 겨룰 수 있는 공정한 기회를 주다 (= level the playing field; compete on a level playing field; compete with others to prove oneself)

  - pit ~ against someone: ~을 아무개와 겨루다

  - compete to prove oneself: 자신의 능력을 입증하기 위해 경쟁하다 (= do oneself justice)

- without any privileged family background being a deciding factor in success: 어떤 특별한 가정 배경이 성공의 결정적 요인이 되지 않고

  - any privileged family background: 특권을 누리는 가정 배경

  - a deciding factor: ~에 결정적 요인 (= a critical factor in)

3. 그러나 지금 우리 사회 구석구석의 모습은 우리 사회가 진정한 경쟁사회가 아님을 보여준다.

>>> (a) However, from what we see happening across Korea now, Korea still has a long way to go before it can be called a truly competitive society.

- **from what we see happening:** 우리들 눈 앞에서 일어나는 일을 보면 (= as it stands; as things stand; the way I see it; with the situation the way it is; with the reality as it is)

- **across Korea:** 한국 곳곳에

- **Korea still has a long way to go before it can be called a truly competitive society:** 한국이 참다운 경쟁사회로 보기에는 아직도 멀었다

  - **have a long way to go:** ~하기에는 아직도 멀다

>>> (b) However, what is happening in Korea shows that as yet Korea is not a truly competitive society.

- **as yet Korea is not a truly competitive society:** 한국은 아직 참다운 경쟁 사회 가 아니다 (= Korea is far from competitive; Korea is a far cry from a competitive society; Korea is nowhere near fairly competitive)

 관련 유용 표현

1. 내가 들은 바에 의하면 옆집 젊은 부부가 어린 자녀들 때문에 그들의 결혼 생활을 유지하기 위해 애를 썼으나 서로의 입장이 달라 드디어 이혼 소송을 하기로 결정하였다.

  - 내가 들은 바에 의하면: from what I heard
  - 옆집 젊은 부부: the young couple next door
  - 어린 자녀들 때문에: for their small children's sake
  - 그들은 결혼 생활을 유지하기 위해 애쓰다: struggle to stay married; to save their marriage

- 서로의 입장이 다르기 때문에: due to irreconcilable differences
- 이혼 소송을 하다: file for divorce
- ~하기로 결정하다: decide to do

>>> From what I heard, the young couple next door, who have recently been struggling to stay married for their small children's sake, have finally decided to file for divorce.

2. 그 응시자는 인터뷰할 때 본인이 두 가지 외국어를 구사한다는 점을 내세워 취업에 성공할 수 있었다.

- 인터뷰할 때: in the job interview
- 두 가지 외국어를 구사하다: speak two different languages
- 점을 내세워: using/ turning ~ to one's advantage
- 취업에 성공하다: be hired

>>> (a) The applicant is hired because in the job interview he used to his advantage his ability to speak two different languages.

(b) The applicant is hired because in the interview he said his ability to handle two different languages is really his forte.

(c) He is hired because he told the interviewers he can speak two different languages.

Part 4

교육

27

한국인의 호칭

A 번역과 영작

외국어를 학습하는 사람들은 일반적으로 해당 언어의 문법과 발음을 가장 중요한 영역으로 여겨 중점적으로 익히려 한다. 반면 호칭은 비교적 간단하게 생각하고 편리한 대로 사용하는 경향이 있다. 그렇게 호칭을 사용하게 될 경우 예절에 어긋나는 일들이 자주 발생하게 된다. 특히 서로 간의 사회적 위치를 분명히 해야 하는 한국 사회의 특징과 호칭어가 발달한 언어 습관을 고려할 때 호칭 문제는 쉽게 간과할 수 없는 언어예절의 하나이다.

(동아일보 인사이드 코리아 2012.03.30.)

* * *

Foreign language learners in general tend to focus exclusively on grammars and pronunciation, which they consider to be the most important part of the target language.

On the other hand, they treat the title as something relatively simple enough to be dealt with in their convenient way.

However, using the forms of address in such a casual manner would often constitute a breach of etiquette.

For instance, given the unique characteristics of Korean society, where the people normally get their social position clearly stated and the common use of the language, which is characterized by the highly developed styles of address systems, the use of designation in Korean is truly reflective of linguistic etiquette, which is not to be overlooked so easily.

 해설

1. 외국어를 학습하는 사람들은 일반적으로 해당 언어의 문법과 발음을 가장 중요한 영역으로 여겨 중점적으로 익히려 한다.

>>> Foreign language learners in general tend to focus exclusively on grammars and pronunciation, which they consider to be the most important part of the target language.

• foreign language learners in general: 일반적으로 외국어를 학습하는 사람들

　• foreign language: 외국어

　　cf second language: 제2언어, 모국어 외에 국가에서 공용으로 쓰이는 언어

　(예) 싱가포르와 인도에서의 영어

- **in general**: 일반적으로 (= generally; by and large)

- **tend to focus exclusively on grammars and pronunciation**: 문법이나 발음에 주로 집중하는 경향이 있다

- **exclusively**: 전적으로 (= mainly; primarily)

- **focus on**: (관심, 능력을) ~에 집중하다 (= pay attention to)

- **, which they consider to be the most important part of the target language**: 외국어 학습자들은 문법과 발음을 해당 언어의 가장 중요한 영역으로 여긴다

- **consider A to be**: A를 ~으로 여기다 (= A is deemed to be; regard A as)

- **a part of**: ~의 일부

- **the target language**: 해당 언어, 학습 목표로 삼는 언어

  cf 모국어: native language; first language; native tongue; mother tongue

2. 반면 호칭은 비교적 간단하게 생각하고 편리한 대로 사용하는 경향이 있다.

>>> On the other hand, they treat the title as something relatively simple enough to be dealt with in their convenient way.

- **on the other hand**: 반면에 (= at the same time)

- **they treat the title as something**: 그들은 호칭을 ~처럼 취급하다 **cf** take/ treat the title lightly: 호칭을 가볍게 취급하다)

- **treat A as B**: A를 B처럼 취급하다 (= deal with)

- **the title**: 호칭 (= mode of address; a designation; an appellation; forms of address

- **something relatively simple enough to be dealt with in their convenient way**: 그들의 편의에 따라 취급할 만큼 비교적 간단한 것

- **deal with**: ~을 처리하다, 다루다 (= treat)

- **in their convenient way**: 그들이 편리한 방식대로 (= in their own way; as they please)

3. 그렇게 호칭을 사용하게 될 경우 예절에 어긋나는 일들이 자주 발생하게 된다.

>>> However, using the forms of address in such a casual manner would often constitute a breach of etiquette.

- **in such a casual manner**: 대충 그런 식으로 (= in such an easy way)
- **constitute a breach of etiquette**: 예의에 어긋나다 (= violate/ break the rules of etiquette)
- **constitute**: (어떤 행위가) ~으로 간주되다 (= be considered to be)
- **a breach of etiquette**: 예의에서 벗어남 **cf** **a breach of contract**: 계약 위반

4. 특히 서로 간의 사회적 위치를 분명히 해야 하는 한국 사회의 특징과 호칭어가 발달한 언어 습관을 고려할 때 호칭 문제는 쉽게 간과할 수 없는 언어예절의 하나이다.

>>> For instance, given the unique characteristics of Korean society, where the people normally get their social position clearly stated and the common use of the language, which is characterized by the highly developed styles of address systems, the use of designation in Korean is truly reflective of linguistic etiquette, which is not to be overlooked so easily.

- **given the unique characteristics of Korean society**: 한국 사회의 특징을 고려할 때
  - **given**: ~을 고려할 때, 감안할 때 (= considering; taking into account)
  - **the characteristics of**: ~의 특성
- **clearly state social position**: 사회적 위치를 분명히 언급하다
- **the common use of the language**: 그 언어의 공용
- **be characterized by**: ~으로 특징을 짓다 (= be marked by)

- **the highly developed styles of the address system:** 매우 발달한 호칭 방법
  - **style of address:** 호칭 (= mode/ form of address)
- **the use of designation in Korean:** 한국어의 호칭 사용
- **be reflective of linguistic etiquette:** 언어 예절을 반영하다
  - **be reflective of:** ~을 반영하다 (= reflect; show)
- **easily overlooked:** ~을 쉽게 간과하다 (= make light of)

C 관련 유용 표현

1. 나이가 든 여성들이 그들의 꿈을 추구해 신체적 한계를 극복하려고 노력하는 모습은 정말 대단하다. 미국의 한 여성 노인은 68세의 나이에 위험을 무릅쓰고 용감하게 플로리다 해협에서 쿠바까지 수영하여 건너갔는가 하면, 다른 여성은 64세에 마라톤 경주에 출전했다. 또 어떤 노인은 94세에 미 서부에서 동부까지 단독 비행으로 대륙 횡단에 성공하였다.

- 연로한 여성: elderly women
- 그들의 꿈을 추구하여: in the pursuit of their dreams (= pursuing their dreams)
- 그들의 육체적 한계를 극복하다: overcome their physical limitations; challenge/ defy their physical limitations)
- ~은 정말 대단하다: it's really amazing how
- 위험을 무릅쓰고 ~을 하다: take the risk of doing
- ~을 하는데 용감하다: be bold enough to do
- A에서 B까지 수영을 하여 건너가다: swim across from A to B
- 마라톤 경주에 출전하다: participate in the marathon match; take part in the marathon match

- 94세의 노령에: at the advanced age of 94

- 서부에서 동부까지: from the West to the East coast

- 비행으로 미대륙을 횡단하는데 성공하다: successfully fly a plane across America

- ~을 단독으로 하다: do something solo

>>> It's amazing how hard some of the elderly women try to overcome their physical limitations in the pursuit of their dream. Recently, an American woman at age 68 was bold enough to take the risk of swimming across the ocean from Florida to Cuba, another woman aged 64 participated in the full marathon match and still another at the advanced age of 94 successfully flew a plane solo across America from the West coast to the East.

2. 그는 10월까지 프로젝트를 마치기로 하였으나 마감일을 훨씬 넘기고도 연락이 없는데 이는 우리 회사와의 계약 위반이다.

- 그는 10월까지 프로젝트를 마치기로 하였다: He was supposed to have a project completed by October.

- 마감일을 훨씬 넘기다: delay the project far beyond the deadline

- 연락이 없이: without any reasons given for

- 계약 위반이다: be in breach of a contract (= break/ violate a contract; constitute a breach of)

>>> Under the terms of the contract with our company he was supposed to have a project completed by October, but he is now in breach of the contract by delaying the project far beyond the deadline without any reasons given for the failure.

28

과학 기술의 발전

　우리는 어제까지만 해도 신기하다고 감탄했던 제품들이 오늘에는 고물이 되어 버리고 내일에는 또 어떤 제품이 나와 사람들을 깜짝 놀라게 할지 모를 급변하는 사회 속에서 살고 있다. 우리의 생활을 편하게 만드는 과학은 끝없이 진보하여 그 한계가 어디까지인지 예측할 수 없다. 과학이 발달하고 컴퓨터, 인터넷이 영리할수록 인간은 더욱 바쁘고 불안해진다.

＊＊＊

　We are living in an age in which the pace of technological change is so rapid that some new products, which had been touted as being innovative and marvelous until as recently as yesterday, are already getting outdated today, with something perhaps even more amazing expected to hit the shelves tomorrow.

Advances in modern technology, which make our lives so convenient, are such that it is hard to predict just how far this technology can go.

Ultimately, however, the more quickly technology evolves and the smarter the computer and the Internet get, the busier and uneasier people will become.

 해설

1. 우리는 어제까지만 해도 신기하다고 감탄했던 제품들이 오늘에는 고물이 되어 버리고 내일에는 또 어떤 제품이 나와 사람들을 깜짝 놀라게 할지 모를 급변하는 사회 속에서 살고 있다.

>>> We are living in an age in which the pace of technological change is so rapid that some new products, which had been touted as being innovative and marvelous until as recently as yesterday, are already getting outdated today, with something perhaps even more amazing expected to hit the shelves tomorrow.

- **live in an age in which:** ~하는 시대에 살다 (= live in an era when)
- **the pace of technological change:** 과학 기술 변화의 속도
    - **the pace of:** ~의 속도 (= the speed/ rate of)
- **something is so rapid that:** 뭔가가 그처럼 빠르기 때문에 ~하게 되다
- **new products:** 새로운 상품
- **be touted as:** ~하다고 절찬을 받다 (= be billed as)

- **innovative and marvelous**: 혁신적이고 놀라운

- **until as recently as yesterday**: 어제까지만 해도

- **get outdated**: 구식이다 (= be old-fashioned; go out of style)

- **be expected to hit the shelves**: 새 상품 출고가 예상되다 (= be expected to be introduced; be debuted; be rolled out)

- **hit the shelves**: 새로 나오다 (= hit markets)
  [cf] **be on the way**: 새 상품이 출시 예정이다, **roll out**: 새 상품이 나오다

2. 우리의 생활을 편하게 만드는 과학은 끝없이 진보하여 그 한계가 어디까지인지 예측할 수 없다.

>>> Advances in modern technology, which makes our lives so convenient, are such that it is hard to predict just how far this technology can go.

- **advances in modern technology**: 현대 과학 기술의 발전

- **such that**: ~할 정도다

- **it is difficult to predict how far this technology can go**: 이 과학이 얼마나 발전할 수 있을지 예측하기가 힘들다 (= It is hard to predict the extent to which this technology will keep developing; It is difficult to tell when this technological development will end.)

  - **the extent to which**: ~하는 정도 (= the degree to which)

3. 과학이 발달하고 컴퓨터, 인터넷이 영리할수록 인간은 더욱 바쁘고 불안해진다.

>>> Ultimately, however, the more quickly technology evolves and the smarter the computer and the Internet get, the busier and uneasier people will become.

- **the more quickly ~, the busier ~:** ~이 빠르면 빠를 수록 ~이 더욱 바쁘게 되다

- **evolve:** 발전하다 (= develop; advance)

- **become/ get busy and uneasy:** 바쁘고 불안하다

관련 유용 표현

1. 최근에 살인 사건이 매우 흔하게 발생하여 때로는 세상이 어떻게 될 것인가 하는 생각이 든다.

- 최근에: in recent years
- 살인 사건: committing murder; murder case
- 매우 흔하게 발생하여: be such a common occurrence that
  - a common occurrence: 흔히 일어나는 것
- 세상이 어떻게 될 것인가: What is the world coming to (= What the hell is going on in the world?/ What's happening to this world?)
- 생각이 든다: one wonders that

>>> In recent years committing murder is such a common occurrence that one sometimes wonders what the world is coming to.

2. 다이어트하려고 강하게 마음 먹을수록 맛있는 음식이 더 많이 보이니 이상한 노릇이다.

- 다이어트 하려고 강하게 마음 먹을수록: the harder you try to go on a diet
- go on a diet: 다이어트 하다
  cf I'm on a diet: 나는 다이어트중이다.

- 맛있는 음식이 더 많이 보이다: the more delicious food catches my eye
- catch one's eye: 아무의 시선을 끌다 (= look tempting; call one's attention to)
  - be tempting: 구미가 당기다
- 이상한 노릇이다: it's interesting that

>>> It is interesting that the harder I try to go on a diet, the more delicious food catches my eye.

29

대학의 국제 경쟁력

A

번역과 영작

대학은 새로운 지식을 창출하고, 연구 협력을 통해 새로운 지식을 공유하며, 교육을 통해 이를 차세대에 전수하는 지식의 허브여야 한다. 각국이 고등교육 정책의 첫 번째 과제로 세계적 명문대 육성을 꼽는 것도 대학이 국가경쟁력의 원천이 될 수 있다는 판단 때문이다.

(중앙일보 사설 2012.10.09.)

＊ ＊ ＊

Universities are supposed to be a "knowledge hub," where new knowledge is acquired, where it is freely shared through research collaboration, and where it is disseminated to the next generation through education.

Moreover, universities are deemed to be the source of national competitiveness, which is why most countries have adopted a higher education policy aimed primarily at getting their universities built into some of the world's leading academic institutions.

1. 대학은 새로운 지식을 창출하고, 연구 협력을 통해 새로운 지식을 공유하며, 교육을 통해 이를 차세대에 전수하는 지식의 허브여야 한다.

>>> Universities are supposed to be a "knowledge hub," where new knowledge is acquired, where it is freely shared through research collaboration, and where it is disseminated to the next generation through education.

- **be supposed to be/ do:** (규칙·습관에 따라) ~을 하기로 되어 있다
- **acquire knowledge:** 지식을 얻다 (= gain knowledge)
- **share knowledge:** 지식을 나누다
- **through research collaboration:** 연구 협력을 통해
- **disseminate knowledge to:** 지식을 ~에게 전수하다 (= impart/ spread/ transfer knowledge to)

2. 각국이 고등교육 정책의 첫 번째 과제로 세계적 명문대 육성을 꼽는 것도 대학이 국가경쟁력의 원천이 될 수 있다는 판단 때문이다.

>>> Moreover, universities are deemed to be the source of national competitiveness, which is why most countries have adopted a higher education policy aimed primarily at getting their universities built into some of the world's leading academic institutions.

- **moreover:** 더욱이 (= furthermore; in addition)

- **be deemed to be:** ~으로 간주되다, 여겨지다 (= be considered to be)

- **the source of:** ~의 원천

- **national competitiveness:** 국가 경쟁력

- **, which is why:** 그렇기 때문에 ~을 하다 (= which is the reason that)

- **adopt a policy:** 정책을 채택하다

- **a higher education policy:** 고등교육 정책 (= a policy on higher education)

- **a policy aimed at:** ~하는 것을 목표로 삼는 정책

- **get their universities built into:** 그들의 대학을 ~가 되게 하다

  - **build up A into B:** A를 B로 발전시키다 (= develop/ grow A into B; get A grown into B)

- **get something to be done:** ~로 되게끔 하다

- **the world's leading academic institutions:** 세계적 명문 교육기관

관련 유용 표현

1. 미국 대학에서 공부하는 많은 외국인 학생들은 영어에 익숙하지 못한 것 같다. 그래서 특정한 주제에 관해 논문을 요구하는 과목은 매우 힘들다고 생각한다.

- 미국 대학에서 공부하는 외국인 학생: foreign students studying at American universities
- ~한 것 같다: seem to do/ be
- 영어에 익숙하다: be proficient in English (= be good at English)
- 어느 특정한 주제에 관한 논문을 요구하다: require writing papers on a particular subject
- ~을 써야 하는 과목: courses requiring writing (papers)

- 과목을 수강하다: take a course
- ~하기가 매우 힘들다고 생각하다: find it very difficult to do

>>> Many foreign students studying at American universities do not seem to be highly proficient in English, which is why they find it very difficult to take any academic courses requiring a lot of writing on a particular subject.

2. 영어를 구사한다는 것이 개인에게 있어 큰 경쟁력이었으나 훌륭한 번역 프로그램이 출시되니 그런 생각이 바뀔 때가 되었다.

- 영어를 구사하는 것이 개인에게 큰 경쟁력이 되었다: a high level of proficiency in English has been a good competitive edge for the speaker
- 훌륭한 번역 프로그램이 출시되니: with the introduction of a good translation program
- 생각이 바뀔 때가 되었다: it's high time we changed the view; it's about time we changed the view

>>> A high level of proficiency in English has often been considered to be a good competitive edge for the speakers, but with the introduction of a good translation program, it's high time we changed the view.

③ 어린이의 어휘력 향상

A 번역과 영작

자녀들도 어휘력을 높이기 위해서 책을 많이 읽어야 한다는 것을 대부분 다 안다. 하지만 그 중요성에도 불구하고 실천이 안 되는 게 현실이다. 역시 학년과 연령에 관계없이 학부모를 대상으로 하는 수많은 세미나에서 반드시 독서가 강조되는 것은 그 만큼 독서가 자녀의 학업 성적은 물론이고 인격 성장에 가장 중요한 역할을 하기 때문이다. 전문가들은 책, 잡지, 신문과 자주 접하는 가정 환경에서 자란 자녀들은 그렇지 않은 자녀보다 훨씬 좋은 성적을 받는다고 말한다.

(중앙일보 2012.07.15.)

* * *

Most people know perfectly well that children should also read a lot of books in order to expand their vocabulary. The reality, however, is that fewer children do despite the importance of reading.

Therefore, the reason why reading is the main focus of attention at a number of seminars held for the parents, regardless of the grade and age of their children, is because it plays a key role in shaping children's character, as well as improving their grades in school.

Reading specialists thus claim that children, who are brought up in a family environment where there are a wide variety of books, magazines and newspapers readily available to them, are far more likely to get better grades than those left without easy access to such resources.

 해설

1. 자녀들도 어휘력을 높이기 위해서 책을 많이 읽어야 한다는 것을 대부분 다 안다. 하지만 그 중요성에도 불구하고 실천이 안 되는 게 현실이다.

>>> Most people know perfectly well that children should also read a lot of books in order to expand their vocabulary. The reality, however, is that fewer children do despite the importance of reading.

- **most people know perfectly well that**: 대부분 ~을 잘 알고 있다 (= … know fully well that~)
- **read a lot of books**: 책을 많이 읽다 (= do a lot of reading)
- **expand one's vocabulary**: 어휘력을 키우다 (= enrich/ improve one's vocabulary)
- **the reality is that**: 현실이 ~이다

• **despite the importance**: 그 중요성에도 불구하고 (= in spite of the importance)

2. 역시 학년과 연령에 관계없이 학부모를 대상으로 하는 수많은 세미나에서 반드시 독서가 강조되는 것은 그 만큼 독서가 자녀의 학업 성적은 물론이고 인격 성장에 가장 중요한 역할을 하기 때문이다.

>>> Therefore, the reason why reading is the main focus of attention at a number of seminars held for the parents, regardless of the grade and age of their children, is because it plays a key role in shaping children's character, as well as improving their grades in school.

• **the main focus of attention**: 관심의 초점

   • **draw attention to**: ~로 관심을 돌리다 (= turn attention to)

• **a number of**: 많은

• **a seminar held for**: ~를 위한 세미나

• **regardless of**: ~에 상관 없이 (= irrespective of)

• **play a role in doing**: ~을 하는 역할을 하다 (= help do)

• **shape character**: 인격을 함양하다 (= build/ form character)

• **improve grades in school**: 학교 성적을 올리다

3. 전문가들은 책, 잡지, 신문과 자주 접하는 가정 환경에서 자란 자녀들은 그렇지 않은 자녀보다 훨씬 좋은 성적을 받는다고 말한다.

>>> Reading specialists thus claim that children, who are brought up in a family environment where there are a wide variety of books, magazines and newspapers readily available to them, are far more likely to get better grades than those left without easy access to such resources.

- **bring up:** 아이를 키우다 (= raise; rear)

- **a family environment, where there are:** ~이 있는 가정 환경

- **a variety of:** 다양한

- **be available to:** ~에 접할 수 있다 (= be made (readily) accessible to)

- **be left without easy access to:** ~에 쉽게 접할 수 없는 처지에 있다 (= be deprived of)

 C 관련 유용 표현

1. 대부분의 한국 학생들이 영어 공부에 많은 시간을 소비하는 이유는 영어 능력을 갖춘 사람
   은 일반적으로 원하는 대학에 입학하거나 좋은 직업과 승진할 수 있는 기회를 더 얻을 수 있
   기 때문이다.

   - 영어 공부에 많은 시간을 소비하다: spend a lot of time on learning English
   - 이유는 ~이다: the reason (why) ~ is because/ that
   - 원하는 대학에 입학할 수 있는 기회를 얻다: get a chance to get into a university of one's
     choice
       - a university of one's choice: 원하는 대학
   - 좋은 직업을 구하다: get a good job
   - 승진할 기회를 얻다: get an opportunity for career advancement

   >>> The reason most Korean students spend so much time on learning
   English is because those equipped with the English skills normally get
   a better chance to get into a university of their choice, get a good job
   and have an opportunity for career advancement.

2. 나이, 성별, 연령에 관계없이 건강 문제는 가장 중요한 관심거리이다.

- 나이 성별에 관계없이: regardless of age or gender

- 건강 문제는 가장 중요한 관심거리이다: Health is an important issue for all

>>> Health is an important issue for all, regardless of age or gender.

삶과 인문학

번역과 영작

인문학은 인간에 관한 학(學)이라고 하지만, 일반적으로 읽고 생각하고, 대화하고, 쓰는 일과 관련된 학문이다. 문학, 역사, 철학은 지금 여기에서 인간다운 삶을 이루어가기 위해 필요한 능력을 함양하고자 한다. 이 능력이 결여되면 어떤 사회가 될 것인가? 방향을 잃은 채 오직 동물적 탐욕에 사로잡혀 맹목적 생명 유지에 집착하는 야만 사회가 될 것이다.

(중앙일보 2012.11.15.)

* * *

Although the humanities are defined as a study of humans, they are in general closely related to the academic study dealing with reading, thinking, conversing and writing.

Literature, history and philosophy are the basic subjects aimed at developing the necessary ability of the people to live the kind of life they deserve in the here and now.

Naturally, you may wonder what kind of society ours would be like without such an ability.

It would then most likely be a savage society, where people, lacking direction and being consumed with animal instincts, are preoccupied with merely maintaining their life.

 해설

1. 인문학은 인간에 관한 학(學)이라고 하지만, 일반적으로 읽고 생각하고, 대화하고, 쓰는 일과 관련된 학문이다.

>>> Although the humanities are defined as a study of humans, they are in general closely related to the academic study dealing with reading, thinking, conversing and writing.

- **be defined as:** ~으로 정의하다
- **a study of humans:** 인간에 관한 연구
    - **be related to:** ~과 관련되다
- **academic study:** 학문
- **deal with:** (주제, 소재로) ~을 다루다 (= be concerned with; be about)

2. 문학, 역사, 철학은 지금 여기에서 인간다운 삶을 이루어가기 위해 필요한 능력을 함양하고
   자 한다.

>>> Literature, history and philosophy are the basic subjects aimed at
developing the necessary ability of the people to live the kind of life
they deserve in the here and now.

- (be) aimed at: ~을 목표로 하다
- develop the ability of the people to do: ~을 할 수 있는 인간의 능력을 키우다
- live the kind of life they deserve: 인간이 살 만한 삶을 살다 (= live like humans; live
  the kind of life that is worthy of humans; live life as they should; live life befitting
  human beings)
    - deserve: ~을 누릴 자격이 있다
    - be worthy of: ~에게 어울리는
- in the here and now: 지금, 여기에 (= at present)

3. 이 능력이 결여되면 어떤 사회가 될 것인가? 방향을 잃은 채 오직 동물적 탐욕에 사로잡혀 맹
   목적 생명 유지에 집착하는 야만 사회가 될 것이다.

>>> Naturally, you may wonder what kind of society ours would be like
without such an ability. It would then most likely be a savage society,
where people, lacking direction and being consumed with animal
instincts, are preoccupied with merely maintaining their life.

- you may wonder what: ~인지 궁금할 것이다
- ours = our society
- be like: ~과 같다 **cf** What is it like?: 그것이 어떻게 생겼는가?

- **savage society**: 야만 사회
- **lack direction**: 방향을 잃다
  - **lack ideas/ confidence**: 아이디어가/ 자신이 없다
- **be consumed with**: (어떤 감정에) 사로 잡히다
- **animal instincts**: 동물적 본능
- **be preoccupied with**: ~에 정신이 팔리다 (= be obsessed with)
- **maintain their life**: 그들의 생명을 유지하다

C 관련 유용 표현

1. 새로운 교육제도는 학생들의 암기 학습을 권장하기 보다 문제를 해결할 수 있는 창의적 능력 개발을 목표로 해야 할 것이다.

- 새로운 교육 제도: the new educational system (= the new policy on education)
- 암기 학습을 권장하다: encourage rote learning
- 문제를 해결할 수 있는 창의적 능력 개발을 목표로 하다: aim at developing the creative ability to solve problems
  - develop the ability to do: ~을 할 수 있는 능력을 개발하다
  - solve problems: 문제를 해결하다
  - ~하는 것을 목표로 하다: aim at doing

>>> The new educational system should be aimed at developing the creative ability of the students to solve problems instead of just encouraging rote learning

2. 문학, 역사 등에 관한 독서를 하지 않고서는 무언가 생각하고 글을 쓰는 과제를 잘 하기는 불가능하다.

- 문학과 역사에 관한 독서를 하다: read major works of literature and history books
- 독서를 하지 않고서는: without reading
- 생각하다: do thinking
- 글을 쓰다: do writing

>>> It is hardly possible to do critical thinking and writing without reading major works of literature and history books.

32 일본 대학생의 해외연수 기피

A 번역과 영작

　일본 대학생의 해외유학 기피 풍조는 일본 기업의 채용문화와도 관련이 있다. 일본에서는 석사나 박사 학위 취득이 아닌 1, 2년 단기 유학의 경우 오히려 취직하는 데 마이너스다. 일본 기업들은 4년 정규과정을 마치고 제때 졸업한 학생을 더 선호가 때문이다. 인구 1억 2,000만 명이 넘는 든든한 내수시장이 있어 기업들이 해외 시장을 적극적으로 개척할 필요성이 떨어지는 것도 한 요인이다. 하지만 일본 경제 침체가 20년 넘게 이어지면서 상황이 바뀌었다.

(동아닷컴 2012.03.26.)

* * *

　The growing reluctance by the Japanese college students to study abroad has something to do with the employment culture within the Japanese corporations.

　In Japan, for instance, those who have just taken short-term courses abroad like one-or-two year educational programs without receiving Ph.D. or M.A. might be put rather at a disadvantage when it comes to seeking employment.

Moreover, the Japanese companies apparently prefer to hire those who have successfully completed the regular 4-year college course on time. Plus the strong domestic markets, with a population of more than 120 million, practically obviate the need to actively make inroads into the global markets.

Today, however, the situation has changed after more than 20 years of deep economic recession Japan has been suffering.

B 해설

1. 일본 대학생의 해외유학 기피 풍조는 일본 기업의 채용문화와도 관련이 있다.

>>> (a) The growing reluctance by the Japanese college students to study abroad has something to do with the employment culture within the Japanese corporations.

- the reluctance by someone to do: 아무개의 주저함, 꺼려함 (= the unwillingness shown by someone) cf someone is reluctant to do
- by the Japanese college students: 일본 대학생들에 의한 (= on the part of the Japanesecollege students; among/ of the Japanese college students)

- **study abroad**: 해외유학을 하다

- **have something to do with**: ~과 관계가 있다 (= be somewhat related to)

- **the employment culture within the Japanese corporations**: 일본 기업 내의 채용 문화

>>> **(b)** There is a possible link between an unwillingness shown by the Japanese students to study abroad and the employment culture within the Japanese corporations.

cf conglomerate: 대기업

- **there is a link between A and B**: A와 B 사이에 관계가 있다.

2. 일본에서는 석사나 박사 학위 취득이 아닌 1, 2년 단기 유학의 경우 오히려 취직하는 데 마이너스다.

>>> **(a)** In Japan those who have just taken short-term courses abroad like one-or-two year educational programs without receiving Ph.D. or M.A. might be put rather at a disadvantage when it comes to seeking employment.

- **take short-term courses abroad**: 해외에서 단기 과정을 밟다

- **be put at a disadvantage**: 불리하게 되다 (= be a handicap; count against)

- **when it comes to seeking employment**: 일자리를 찾는 데 있어서 (= when it comes to finding jobs)

    - **when it comes to doing**: ~하는 것으로 말하면

    - **seek employment**: 일자리를 찾다 (= look for jobs; go after jobs; snag jobs; be gunning for jobs)

>>> (b) For instance, in Japan, without Ph.D. and M.A. obtained from abroad, just taking short-term courses abroad such as one-or-two year academic programs could be a handicap to an effort to find jobs.

- **a handicap to:** ~에 불리한 조건 (= a minus)
- **an effort to do:** ~을 하려는 노력

3. 일본 기업들은 4년 정규과정을 마치고 제때 졸업한 학생을 더 선호하기 때문이다. 인구 1억 2000만 명이 넘는 든든한 내수시장이 있어 기업들이 해외 시장을 적극적으로 개척할 필요성이 떨어지는 것도 한 요인이다.

>>> Moreover, the Japanese companies apparently prefer to hire those who have successfully completed the regular 4-year college course on time. Plus the strong domestic markets with a population of more than 120 million practically obviate the need to actively make inroads into the global markets.

- **moreover:** 게다가, 뿐만 아니라 (= furthermore)
- **prefer to do:** ~하기를 더 좋아하다 (= would rather do)
- **hire someone:** 아무개를 고용하다 (= give a job to someone; employ someone)
- **successfully complete the regular 4-year college courses on time:** 4년제 대학 정규 과정을 제 기간에 마치다 (= graduate from a university on time)
- **on time:** 제때에/ 제시간에
- **the strong domestic markets with a population of more than 120 million:** 인구 1억 2천만명 이상 되는 튼튼한 국내 시장
- **obviate the need to do:** ~할 필요성을 없애다 (= do not make it necessary to do; do not need to do)

- **make inroads into the global markets**: 해외시장을 개척하다, 침식하다 (= get into/ break into the global markets/ tap into the global markets)

4. 하지만 일본 경제 침체가 20년 넘게 이어지면서 상황이 바뀌었다.

>>> Today, however, the situation has changed after more than 20 years of deep economic recession Japan has been suffering.

- **The situation has changed.** 상황이 바뀌었다. (= Things have changed.)
  cf **Times have changed.** 시대가 바뀌었다.
- **Japan has been suffering economic recession.** 일본이 경제 침체에 빠지다.
  (= going through economic recession; experiencing economic recession)

 관련 유용 표현

1. 요즘 많은 대학 졸업생들이 구직에 거듭 실패하면서 그들이 실무 경력이 없는 것이 큰 장애가 된다고 한다. 하지만 그들은 일할 수 있는 기회도 없이 어떻게 실무 경험을 쌓을 수 있느냐는 것이다.

- 요즘: in recent times; nowadays
- 구직에 거듭 실패하면서: after continual failure to land/ find a job)
  - failure to do: ~을 못함
- 실무 경력 부족: lack of practical experience
  - lack of: ~의 부족
  - practical experience: 실무 경력, 실제 경험

- 일자리를 구하는 데: when it comes to seeking employment

- seek employment: 직업을 찾다

- ~에 장애가 되다: be a handicap (= be put/ placed at a disadvantage)

- 그들은 ~의 의문을 제기한다: They then raise the question of

- 경험을 얻다: have experience under one's belt; gain experience

>>> In recent times many college graduates, after continual failure to land a job, find that their lack of practical experience is a big handicap when it comes to seeking employment. They then raise the question of how they can possibly be expected to have experience under their belt without first getting a chance to work.

2. 현실적으로 말해서 고등교육에서 배우는 것이 업무 수행에 직접 관련이 없어 활용되지 않는다면 그와 같은 교육을 반드시 추구할 필요는 없다.

- 현실적으로 말해서: practically speaking; in practical terms

- 고등 교육: higher education

- ~에서 배우는 것: what you learn from

- 업무 수행에 직접 관련이 있어 활용될 수 있는: be directly related and applicable to the performance of your duty

    - be related to: ~에 관련이 있다

    - be applicable to: ~에 활용, 적용이 되다

    - the performance of duty: 업무 수행

- ~을 추구할 필요가 없다: it's not necessary to pursue

>>> In practical terms, it's not necessary to pursue higher education unless what you learn from your study is directly related and applicable to the performance of your duty.

저출산과 고령화

33

번역과 영작

저출산과 고령화가 지속될 경우 핵심 노동인구의 연령이 높아지고, 생산 가능인구가 줄어든다. 전체 인구의 중간연령(중위연령)은 지난 2010년 37.9세에서 오는 2030년 48.5세로 높아지고, 2040년엔 52.6세까지 올라갈 전망이다. 생산가능인구는 2016년을 정점으로 급격히 줄어들 것으로 예상되고 있다. 이렇게 되면 노동력 부족과 함께 새로운 지식과 기술의 습득 속도가 떨어지면서 생산능력이 저하된다. 노동현장에서의 세대 갈등과 세대간 일자리 다툼이 사회 문제가 될 우려도 있다. 부양할 고령인구의 증가로 건강연금복지비용이 급증해 국가 재정을 옥죄고 성장 잠재력을 떨어뜨릴 우려도 크다.

(중앙일보 오피니언 사설 2012.06.23.)

* * *

If the current low birth rate and process of aging should continue in Korea, the average age of core workers would gradually rise, while the potential productive population is bound to shrink.

The median age of the whole population is projected to rise from 37.9 in 2010 to 48.5 in 2030 and to 50.6 in 2040, with the number of potentially productive workers starting to decline drastically from the peak in 2016.

If the projection holds true, then the level of productivity would fall due to a serious labor shortage coupled with a slow speed at which new information is obtained and high technology is adopted.

As a result, a critical social issue could arise from the generational conflicts in the workplace combined with the fierce competition between the older and younger generation for jobs.

Furthermore, with a steady growth in the number of the aging population requiring full support, there is growing concern that the spiraling cost of healthcare, pension and welfare could put a strain on public finances, thereby reducing potential for economic growth.

1. 저출산과 고령화가 지속될 경우 핵심 노동인구의 연령이 높아지고, 생산 가능인구가 줄어든다.

>>> If the current low birth rate and process of aging should continue in Korea, the average age of core workers would gradually rise, while the potential productive population is bound to shrink.

- the low birth rate: 저출산율
- the process of aging: 고령화 (진행) (= the aging process)
- core worker: 핵심 노동자
- productive population: 생산적 인구
- be bound to do: ~할 가능성이 크다 (= be likely to do)
- shrink: 줄다 (= drop; fall; decline)

2. 전체 인구의 중간연령(중위연령)은 지난 2010년 37.9세에서 오는 2030년 48.5세로 높아지고, 2040년엔 52.6세까지 올라갈 전망이다. 생산가능인구는 2016년을 정점으로 급격히 줄어들 것으로 예상되고 있다.

>>> The median age of the whole population is projected to rise from 37.9 in 2010 to 48.5 in 2030 and to 50.6 in 2040, with the number of potentially productive workers starting to decline drastically from the peak in 2016.

- the median age: 중간 연령

- **be projected to do**: ~할 것으로 예상되다 (= be estimated to do; be predicted to do)

- **rise from A (37.9%) to B (48.5%)**: A에서 B로 상승하다

- **, with A doing**: A가 ~을 하게 되면서 (→ 동시 상황을 나타냄)

  with <u>the number of potentially productive workers</u> starting to decline
  A

3. 이렇게 되면 노동력 부족과 함께 새로운 지식과 기술의 습득 속도가 떨어지면서 생산능력이 저하된다.

>>> If the projection holds true, then the level of productivity would fall due to a serious labor shortage coupled with a slow speed at which new information is obtained and high technology is adopted.

- **if the projection holds true**: 만약 이 예측이 옳다면 (= if so; if the estimate is reliable; if this is the case; if the prediction comes true; if this projection proves correct; if the forecast is right; if the prediction is right on the money)

- **the productivity level would fall**: 생산성의 (수준이) 떨어지다 (= the productivity level would drop/ decline/ go down)

- **due to a labor shortage**: 노동력 부족 때문에

    - **due to**: ~때문에 (= because of)

- **a shortage**: 부족

- **coupled with**: ~과 함께 (= combined with)

- **a slow speed at which new information is obtained and high technology (is) adopted**: 느린 속도의 새로운 지식과 기술 습득

    - **at a slow speed**: 느린 속도로 (= at a slow pace)

    - **obtain information**: 지식을 습득하다

    - **adopt technology**: 기술을 채택하다

4. 노동현장에서의 세대 갈등과 세대간 일자리 다툼이 사회 문제가 될 우려도 있다.

>>> As a result, a critical social issue could arise from the generational conflicts in the workplace combined with the fierce competition between the older and younger generation for jobs.

- a social issue/ problem could arise from: ~때문에 사회문제가 발생할 수 있다
    - arise from: ~에서 유발하다
    - generational conflicts: 세대 갈등
    - be combined with: ~이 결합하다 (= coupled with)
- competition between A and B for C: C를 위한 A와 B의 경쟁
  the fierce competition between the older and younger generation for jobs
                             A   B   C

5. 부양할 고령인구의 증가로 건강연금복지비용이 급증해 국가 재정을 옥죄고 성장 잠재력을 떨어뜨릴 우려도 크다.

>>> Furthermore, with a steady growth in the number of the aging population requiring full support, there is growing concern that the spiraling cost of healthcare, pension and welfare could put a strain on public finances, thereby reducing potential for economic growth.

- with a steady growth in the number of the aging population requiring full support: 부양할 고령인구가 증가하면서 (= as the number of the aging population requiring full support steadily increases)
- there is growing concern that: ~에 대한 우려가 크다 (= there are fears that)
- the spiraling cost of: 늘어나는 ~의 비용

- **healthcare**: 의료서비스

- **put a strain on public finances**: ~에 재정적 압박을 가하다 (= make a big dent in public finances; take a heavy toll on public finances; stretch public finances to the limit; get public finances stretched too thin)

- **thereby**: 그렇게 함으로써

- **reduce potential for growth**: 성장 잠재력을 줄이다

관련 유용 표현

1. 비무장지대에서 북한군의 도발이 빈번해지면서 대부분의 사람들은 그와 같은 의도적 도발이 전면전으로 확대될 가능성에 대해서 걱정한다.

- 비무장지대: the demilitarized zone
- 북한군의 도발행위: the provocative acts committed by North Korean soldiers
- 의도적 도발이 전면전으로 확대될 가능성: the possibility of the deliberate provocation escalating into all-out war
  - the possibility of doing: ~할 가능성
  - deliberate provocation: 의도적 도발
  - escalate into: ~로 확대되다
  - all-out war: 전면전 (= full-scale war)
- ~에 대해 걱정하다: voice/ express/ raise concerns about
- 두 나라 사이: between the two parts of Korea

>>> With the provocative acts often committed by North Korean soldiers along the demilitarized zone in Korea, people in general voice their concerns about the possibility of such deliberate provocation escalating into all-out war in Korea.

2. 저출산 문제의 영향으로 해마다 폐교되는 초등학교가 늘고 있는데 특히 농어촌 지역에서 이 같은 문제가 더 심각하다.

- 저출산(율): a low birth (rate)
- ~의 영향으로: as a result of
- 폐교되는 초등학교가 늘고 있다: the number of the primary school closures keeps growing (= there is an increase in the closure of the primary schools)
- 농어촌지역에서: in the provinces
- 이 같은 문제가 더 심각하다: the situation is even more serious
    - all the more: 더욱 더

>>> As a result of a low birth in Korea, every year the number of the primary school closures keeps growing, especially in the provinces, where the situation is even more serious.

학교 폭력

34

A 번역과 영작

　최근 중학생의 잇단 자살을 통해 드러나 학교폭력의 심각성에 대해 국민들이 큰 충격을 받고 있다. 문제는 학교폭력이 최근 갑자기 발생한 문제가 아니라는 것이다. 우리는 학교폭력이 발생했을 때만 반짝 관심을 갖다가 잠잠해지면 이내 잊어버리는 과정을 반복하고 있다. 국민적 관심이 모아진 지금이야말로 근본적인 해결책을 마련하기 위한 노력이 필요한 시기이다.

　　　　　　　　　　　　　　　　　　　　　　　　　(동아일보 2012.04.23.)

* * *

　Recently, Korean people have been shocked at the gravity of escalating school violence, as evidenced by a series of the violence-related suicides committed by some junior high school students.

　The problem, however, is that the school violence is not something that has recently come out of the blue.

The truth of the matter is that we have been repeating the same patterns of devoting only passing attention to school violence whenever it occurs, quickly forgetting about it as soon as it stops for a while.

Therefore, now is the best time to find ways to deal with the violence once and for all while our attention is being drawn to the act of violence.

 해설

1. 최근 중학생의 잇단 자살을 통해 드러나 학교폭력의 심각성에 대해 국민들이 큰 충격을 받고 있다.

>>> (a) Recently, Korean people have been shocked at the gravity of escalating school violence, as shown by a series of the violence-related suicides committed by some junior high school students.

- **be (deeply) shocked at:** (큰) 충격을 받다 (= be stunned at; be flabbergasted/ nonplussed/ be floored/ be taken aback by/ be dumbfounded by)
  cf **appalled; floor:** 어안이 벙벙하다
- **gravity of:** ~의 심각성 (= seriousness of)
- **, as evidenced by:** ~에 보이듯이 (= as shown/ seen/ revealed/ manifested in)
- **a series of violence:** 잇단 폭력
- **violence-related suicide:** 폭력과 관련된 자살
- **commit a suicide:** 자살하다 (= take/ end one's own life)

>>> (b) In recent times, Koreans have been completely stunned at the increasing level of school violence, as revealed by the number of violence-related suicides involving junior high school students.

- be stunned at: ~에 충격을 받다
- the level of school violence: 학교 폭력의 정도
- suicides involving junior high school students: 중학생들이 관련된 자살
  (= suicides committed by …)

2. 문제는 학교폭력이 최근 갑자기 발생한 문제가 아니라는 것이다.

>>> The problem, however, is that the school violence is not something that has recently come out of the blue.

- the problem is (that): 문제는 ~라는 것이다
  [cf] there's/ here's the rub: ~에 문제가 있다
- be not something that: ~한 것이 아니다
- come out of the blue: 갑자기 생기다
  - out of the blue: 갑자기 (= out of nowhere; all of a sudden)

3. 우리는 학교폭력이 발생했을 때만 반짝 관심을 갖다가 잠잠해지면 이내 잊어버리는 과정을 반복하고 있다.

>>> The truth of the matter is that we have been repeating the same patterns of devoting only passing attention to school violence whenever it occurs, quickly forgetting about it as soon as it stops for a while.

- **the truth of the matter is that**: 실은 ~이 이러이러하다

- **repeat the same pattern of doing**: ~하는 패턴을 되풀이 하다 (= be in the habit of doing; repeat the cycle by doing)

- **devote attention to**: ~에 관심을 갖다 (= pay/ turn/ give attention to)

    - **passing attention**: (잠깐의) 관심 (= fleeting attention)

- **violence occurs**: 폭력이 발생하다 = violence enters/ takes place/ flares)

4. 국민적 관심이 모아진 지금이야말로 근본적인 해결책을 마련하기 위한 노력이 필요한 시기이다.

> >>> Therefore, now is the best time to find ways to deal with the violence once and for all while our attention is being drawn to the act of violence.

- **now is the best time to do**: 지금이야말로 ~하기에 적기다

- **find ways to do**: ~하는 방법을 찾다

- **deal with**: ~을 다루다

- **once and for all**: 최종적으로 (= completely and finally)

- **draw one's attention to**: ~로 주의를 끌다

- **act of violence**: 폭력행위

1. 많은 나라에서 대통령 후보들이 부패 근절을 선거 공약으로 내세움에도 불구하고 새로 당선된 대통령들이 부패 관료들을 권력의 자리에서 퇴출시키지 못해 부패는 아직도 곳곳에서 만연하고 있다.

- 부패를 근절시키겠다는 대통령 후보들의 선거 공약: the campaign pledge by the presidential candidates to root out corruption
  - the campaign pledge: 선거 공약
  - make/ give a pledge to do: ~하겠다는 공약을 하다
  - root out/ eliminate corruption: 부패를 근절하다
- 부패는 곳곳에서 만연하다: Corruption is widespread throughout the places.
  - be widespread: ~이 널리 퍼져있다
- the newly-elected president: 새로 당선된 대통령
- fail to do: ~을 못하다
- 부패 관료들을 권력의 자리에서 퇴출시키다: get the corrupted government officials removed from their positions of power
  - remove A from B: A를 B에서 제거하다, 퇴출시키다
  - position of power: 권력의 자리
  - get something done: ~을 이루다

>>> In many countries, despite the campaign pledge made by the presidential candidates to root out corruption, it is still widespread throughout the places with the newly-elected presidents failing to get the corrupted government officials removed from their positions of power.

2. 노인들이 혼자 살다가 죽어 시간이 한참 지나서야 그 죽음이 알려지는 일이 이어지는 요즘 서
   둘러 노인들의 고독한 삶이라는 문제에 대한 근본적인 해결책을 마련해야 할 것이다.

- 노인들이 혼자 살다: elderly people live alone; some elderly persons lead a lonely life
- 그들의 죽음이 알려지다: They are found dead
- 시간이 한참 지나서야: long after
- 노인들의 고독한 삶이라는 문제 대한 근본적인 해결책을 마련하다: come up with a viable
  solution to the problem of their lonely life
- ~을 해야 하다: it's imperative to do

>>> These days when elderly people, while living alone, are often
found dead long after their death, it is imperative to come up with a
viable solution to the fundamental problem of their lonely life.

35

입시 경쟁 교육

 번역과 영작

일부 학부모들은 국·영·수 공부를 시키지 않고 인성교육을 시키는 교사에 대해 무능한 교사로 낙인찍고 있다. 때문에 교사들은 어쩔 수 없이 인성교육 대신 대학 진학을 위한 교육을 하게 되면서 학교가 학원으로 전락한 것이다. 때문에 입시 경쟁 위주의 학교 사회 환경을 개선하지 않으면 학교 폭력은 계속 유지될 수밖에 없다는 것이 전문가들의 시각이다.

* * *

Nowadays the teachers, who give a character education to the students instead of teaching them core subjects like Korean, English or mathematics, are often labelled by some parents as incompetent ones.

Consequently, the teachers are coming under pressure to sacrifice a character education to prepare them for admission to universities, with the result that the high schools now have been relegated to the role of the private academies.

Thus education leaders today share the view that school violence will be perpetuated unless and until the current school environment, in which attention is primarily focused on competition for university entrance, is substantially improved.

 해설

1. 일부 학부모들은 국·영·수 공부를 시키지 않고 인성교육을 시키는 교사에 대해 무능한 교사로 낙인찍고 있다.

>>> Nowadays the teachers, who give a character education to the students instead of teaching them core subjects like Korean, English or mathematics, are often labelled by some parents as incompetent ones.

- give a character education to: ~에게 인성교육을 시키다
    - character education: 인성교육 (= character building)
- core subjects: 핵심 과목
- label A as B: A를 B라고 낙인 찍다, 부르다 (= brand/ tag/ peg A as B; paint/ describe A as B)
- incompetent teachers: 무능 교사

2. 때문에 교사들은 어쩔 수 없이 인성교육 대신 대학 진학을 위한 교육을 하게 되면서 학교가 학원으로 전락한 것이다.

>>> (a) Consequently, the teachers are coming under pressure to sacrifice a character education to prepare them for admission to universities, with the result that the high schools now have been relegated to the role of the private academies.

- **consequently**: 그 결과 (= as a result; therefore)

- **come/ be under the pressure to do**: ~을 하도록 압력을 받다 (= feel pressured to do)

- **sacrifice something to do**: ~을 하기 위해 무엇을 희생하다 (= do something at the expense of)

- **, with the result that**: 그리하여 어떠한 결과를 가져오다 (= , result in)

- **relegate A to B**: A를 B로 전락시키다 (= downgrade A to B; reduce A to B)

- **the role of**: ~의 역할

- **the private academy**: 학원

>>> (b) Therefore, with the teachers feeling obligated to prepare the students to be accepted to universities at the expense of character building, the high schools have now been downgraded to the private academy level.

- **be/ feel obligated to do**: ~을 할 의무감을 갖다

- **be accepted to/ by a university**: 대학에 합격하다 (= gain admission to a university; get into a university) **cf** **receive a thick envelope**: 대학의 합격 통지를 받다

  - **receive a thin envelope**: 대학의 불합격 통지를 받다

  - **get waitlisted**: 입학대기 통지서를 받다

- at the expense of: ~을 희생하여

- character building: 인격 형성

- downgrade A to B: A를 B로 격하시키다 (= lower A to B; reduce A to B)

  lower the status of the high schools to that of the private academy
                A   B

- **cf** get accepted by a university/ get admitted to a university: 대학에 합격하다

  get rejected by a university/ get a thin envelop from a university. 대학에 떨어지다

3. 때문에 입시 경쟁 위주의 학교 사회 환경을 개선하지 않으면 학교 폭력을 계속 유지될 수밖에 없다는 것이 전문가들의 시각이다.

>>> Thus education leaders today share the view that school violence will be perpetuated unless and until the current school environment, in which attention is primarily focused on competition for university entrance, is substantially improved.

- education leaders: 교육 전문가, 지도자 (= education specialists)

- share the view that: ~에 관한 견해를 같이 하다

  cf what's your take on: ~에 관해서 어떻게 생각하십니까?

- perpetuate violence: 폭력을 지속시키다

- unless and until: ~을 할 때까지는 (→ unless의 강조)

- focus attention on: ~에 주의를 기울이다

- competition for: ~에 대한 경쟁

- university entrance: 대학 입학

- improve environment: 환경을 개선하다 **cf** He worked his way through college. 그는 고학으로 대학을 마쳤다. (= He put himself through college.)

관련 유용 표현

1. 이 세상에서 확실한 것은 죽음과 세금뿐이다.

- 이 세상에서: in this world
- ~외에 확실한 것은 아무 것도 없다: nothing is certain but ~
- 죽음과 세금: death and taxes

>>> In this world nothing is certain but death and taxes.

(Benjamin Franklin)

2. 나는 조국을 위해 죽을 수 있는 생명이 오직 하나 밖에 없다는 것이 유감스러울 뿐이다.

- 조국을 위해 죽을 수 있는 생명: one life to lose for my country
- 하나 밖에 없다: have but one
- 유감스러울 뿐이다: I only regret that

>>> I only regret that I have but one life to lose for my country.

(Nathan Hale)

36

해외연수

번역과 영작

연수는 어느새 형편이 넉넉한 가정의 자녀에만 해당되는 게 아닌 일이 됐다. 특히 대학생에겐 필수 과정처럼 돼버렸다. 남아공이나 필리핀까지 영어권이면 어디나 한국 학생이 퍼져 있다. 보통의 부모에겐 버거운 일이 아닐 수 없다. 1년치 연수 비용은 회사원 평균 연봉에 육박한다. 과외비 열심히 대고 대학 등록금 꼬박꼬박 내주는 게 부모 역할의 끝이 아닌 세상이다.

(중앙일보 2012.07.07.)

＊ ＊ ＊

Nowadays going abroad for language learning is no longer deemed to be the prerogative of the few from the well-to-do families. Rather, it is now regarded as a requirement, especially for the college students.

As a result, Korean students are scattered all over the world where English is used as a first or second language, as in South Africa or in the Philippines.

The overseas study is understandably financially burdensome particularly for the ordinary Korean parents, with the enrolment for the one-year English course costing them nearly as much as what an average worker makes a year at a private company.

The reality of the situation is such that today there is more to the parental roles than just gladly paying on time their kids' school expenses including college tuition and the fees for the private lessons.

 B 해설

1. 연수는 어느새 형편이 넉넉한 가정의 자녀에만 해당되는 게 아닌 일이 됐다. 특히 대학생에 겐 필수 과정처럼 돼버렸다.

>>> Nowadays going abroad for language learning is no longer deemed to be the prerogative of the few from the well-to-do families. Rather, it is now regarded as a requirement, especially for the college students.

• **go abroad for language learning:** 해외 언어연수를 하다

• **the prerogative of the few:** 소수가 갖는 특권 (= the exclusive privilege enjoyed by the few; a luxury of the kids from the wealthy families
  cf **enjoy prerogative:** 특권을 누리다

- **the few from the well-to-do families:** 부유한 가정의 혜택 받은 소수 (= some kids from the affluent families)
  - **the well-to-do family:** 부유한 가정 (= the wealthy/ rich family)
- **rather:** 오히려 (~하는 편이다)
- **a requirement:** 필수 요건 (= a required course; a must)

2. 남아공이나 필리핀까지 영어권이면 어디나 한국 학생이 퍼져 있다.

>>> As a result, Korean students are scattered all over the world where English is used as a first or second language, as in South Africa or in the Philippines.

- **be scattered all over/ around the world:** 전 세계에 퍼져있다
- **English is used as a first or second language:** 영어가 모국어 또는 제2외국어로 사용되다

3. 보통의 부모에겐 버거운 일이 아닐 수 없다. 1년치 연수 비용은 회사원 평균 연봉에 육박한다.

>>> (a) The overseas study is understandably financially burdensome particularly for the ordinary Korean parents, with the enrolment for the one-year English course costing them nearly as much as what an average worker makes a year at a private company.

- **the overseas study is financially burdensome for someone:** 해외 연수는 아무 개에게 재정적인 부담이 되다 (= someone finds the overseas study costly)
- **the ordinary Korean parents:** 보통의 한국 부모들

- the enrolment for the one-year English course: 1년 단위의 영어과정 등록
- cost someone as much as: 아무개에게 ~만큼의 비용이 들다
- what an average worker makes a year: 보통 직장인의 일년 소득

>>> (b) It's no wonder, therefore, that the ordinary Korean parents feel financially burdened, with the tuition fees charged for the one-year English program being nearly equivalent to an annual salary for the typical worker at the private companies.

- it's no wonder that: ~하는 것은 당연하다 (= It's little/ small wonder that; it's not surprising that)
- feel financially burdened: 재정적으로 부담을 느끼다
- charge fees for: ~의 대가로 비용을 부과하다
- be equivalent to: ~과 맞먹는 (= be equal to; approximate)
- annual salary: 연봉

>>> (c) The ordinary Korean parents are thus financially pressured, with the cost of enrolling in the one-year English course amounting close to the equivalent of an annual salary for the average employee at the private companies.

- be pressured: ~의 압박감을 느끼다
- the cost of doing: ~하는 비용
- enroll in: (어떤 과목에) 등록하다
- amount to: (액수가) ~에 달하다

- the equivalent of: ~에 상당하는 것

  cf … with the cost of the one-year English program approximating to an annual salary for an average worker at a company

4. 과외비 열심히 대고 대학 등록금 꼬박꼬박 내주는 게 부모 역할의 끝이 아닌 세상이다.

>>> The reality of the situation is such that today there is more to the parental roles than just gladly paying on time their kids' school expenses including college tuition and the fees for the private lessons.

- **The reality of the situation is such that:** 현실 상황이 이러하므로 ~하다 (= that being the case)

- **There is more to A than B:** A는 B 이상이다 (= A means more than B; A extends beyond B; A includes/ involves/ entails more than B)

  there is more to <u>the parental roles</u> than just <u>gladly paying</u>
                             A   B

  taking on/ assuming the parental roles means more than just gladly paying

- **pay on time their kids' school expenses:** 자녀의 학비를 제 때에 내다

- **the fees for the private lesson:** 과외비

1. 교사들은 자기들 직무가 가르치는 일 외에도 번거로운 행정업무까지 담당해야 하므로 교사의 역할은 학생들에게 특정 과목을 가르치는 것 이상이 된다고 불평한다.

   - 교사직은 행정 업무까지 포함하다: Teachers' jobs involve performing/ doing administrative duties
     - 번거로운 행정 업무: onerous administrative duties
     - involves doing: ~하는 것을 포함하다
   - 교사의 역할은 학생들에게 특정 과목을 가르치는 것 이상이 되다: there is more to the teachers' role than just teaching any particular subjects to the students (= the teachers' role extends beyond teaching any particular subjects to the students)
   - there is more to A than B: A는 B 이상의 것이 되다 (= A extends beyond B)

   >>> With the teachers' jobs involving performing onerous administrative duties as well as teaching, teachers complain that there is more to their role than just teaching any particular subjects to the students.

2. 해외에 거주하는 한인은 2015년 현재 세계 181개국에 718만 4872명이 거주하는 것으로 추산되는데 실로 전 세계 어디에나 한국인이 퍼져있다고 보면 된다.

   - 2015년 현재: as of 2015 (= from 2015)
   - 해외에 거주하는 한인: Koreans living abroad
   - 세계 181개국에 718만4872명이 거주한다: 7,184,872 Koreans establish/ take up permanent residence in 181 different countries
   - ~에 거주하다: take up residence in (= establish residence in; live in; settle)

- ~으로 추산되다: be estimated at (= be put at: stand at)
- 전 세계: all over the world (= all around the world)
- 전 세계 어디에나 한국인이 퍼져있다: Koreans are scattered all over the world
- ~라고 보면 된다: I think we can safely assume that (= we can simply say that)

>>> As of 2015, the number of the Koreans living abroad is estimated at 7,184,872. Therefore, I think we can safely assume that they are scattered all over the world, taking up permanent residence in 181 different countries.

학점 퍼주기

번역과 영작

 학점 퍼주기는 학생과 교수 사이의 누이 좋고 매부 좋은 은밀한 거래다. 교수의 입장에서는 적지 않은 등록금을 내고 학교에 다니는데 어떻게 C 이하의 학점을 줄 수 있을까 싶어지고, 또 학점을 나쁘게 받은 학생들에 의한 교수 강의 평가라는 리턴매치가 걱정되기도 한다. 그뿐 아니라 학점을 짜게 준다는 사실이 알려지면, 그 교수 과목은 기피 과목으로 낙인이 찍혀 폐강될 수도 있다. 그리고 성적 제출 후에는 학점에 만족하지 않는 학생들의 전화와 e메일에 시달리게 된다. 현실이 이렇다 보니 교수가 학점을 짜게 주어야 할 이유가 눈곱만큼도 없다. 더 나아가 학생의 취업까지 생각하면 교수의 학점 퍼주기는 쉽게 합리화되어 버린다.

(동아일보 2012.04.02.)

Professors' giving of inflated grades to their students is alleged to be a secret deal between the former and the latter, a deal often seen as being mutually beneficial to both sides.

For instance, the professors, from their perspective, can't help wondering how they can possibly give any grades lower than C to the students, who have to pay such hefty tuition fees to get a university education.

At the same time, their concern is that they might receive a negative end-of-course evaluation of their lectures from the students who get the poor grades.

Then the professors, if found giving low grades, could end up getting their courses branded as something to be avoided by the students, in which case the offering of those courses is bound to be discontinued.

Furthermore, the professors, soon after awarding the grades to the students, are highly likely to get irritated by the calls and emails from those who are not happy with what they get.

Given the circumstances, there is no reason whatsoever to give the bad grades to any of the students.

The professors thus feel fully justified in being generous with their grades, especially when they have their students in mind for employment.

1. 학점 퍼주기는 학생과 교수 사이의 누이 좋고 매부 좋은 은밀한 거래다.

>>> Professors' giving of inflated grades to their students is alleged to be a secret deal between the former and the latter, a deal often seen as being mutually beneficial to both sides.

- **professors' giving of inflated grades to their students:** 교수들이 학생들에게 주는 부풀린 점수 (= giving inflated grades by professors to their students; the practice of giving inflated grades by professors to their students; giving of inflated grades by professors to their students)
    - **inflated grades:** 부풀린 점수
- **be alleged to be:** ~라고 평판이 나다 (= be reputed to be/ do)
- **a secret deal between A and B:** A와 B 사이의 비밀 거래
- **between the former and the latter:** 전자와 후자 사이에 (= between the two sides)
- **be seen as:** ~로 보이다
- **be mutually beneficial to:** ~에게 서로 유익하다
- **both sides:** 양측, 서로 (= both of them)
    cf **be a win-win (situation):** 서로에게 득이 되는 상황

2. 교수의 입장에서는 적지 않은 등록금을 내고 학교에 다니는데 어떻게 C 이하의 학점을 줄 수 있을까 싶어지고, 또 학점을 나쁘게 받은 학생들에 의한 교수 강의 평가라는 리턴매치가 걱정되기도 한다.

>>> For instance, the professors, from their perspective, can't help wondering how they can possibly give any grades lower than C to the students, who have to pay such hefty tuition fees to get a university education. At the same time, their concern is that they might receive a negative end-of-course evaluation of their lectures from the students who get the poor grades.

- **the professors, from their perspective:** 교수들로서는 (= for their part; from their viewpoint; from their side; from their point of view)

- **can't help doing:** ~을 하지 않을 수 없다 (= cannot but do)

- **wonder how:** ~을 어떻게 할까 생각하다

- **how they can possibly give:** ~을 어떻게 줄 수 있겠는가 (→ ~을 도저히 할 수 없다는 뜻)

- **grades lower than C:** C 이하의 학점 (= grades below C)

- **pay hefty tuition fees:** 비싼 등록금을 내다

- **their concern is:** 그들이 염려하는 것은 ~이다

- receiving a negative end-of-course evaluation of their lectures from the students who might want to get back at the professor for the poor grades they get is giving them cause for concern: 학점을 나쁘게 받은 학생들이 응징으로 교수 강의 평가를 부정적으로 하는 점이 걱정되기도 한다.

  - **end of course:** 학기 말

  - **an evaluation of:** ~의 평가

  - **get back at:** 복수하다 (= get even with; revenge)

  - **give causes for concern:** 걱정 거리가 되다 (= be a cause for concern)

3. 그뿐 아니라 학점을 짜게 준다는 사실이 알려지면, 그 교수 과목은 기피 과목으로 낙인이 찍혀 폐강될 수도 있다.

>>> The professors, if found giving low grades, could then end up getting their courses branded as something to be avoided by the students, in which case the offering of those courses is bound to be discontinued.

- , if found giving low grades: 점수가 짠 것으로 알려지면
    - be found doing: ~하는 것으로 알려지다
- end up doing: ~의 결과로 끝나다 (= result in doing)
- get their courses branded as something: 그들 과목이 ~으로 낙인 찍히다
    - brand A as B: A를 B로 낙인 찍히다 (= label A as B)
- something to be avoided/ shunned by the students: 학생들이 피하는 것 (= to steer clear of something)
- , in which case: 그럴 경우
- the offering of those courses is bound to be discontinued: 그들 과목이 폐강될 가능성이 크다
    - the offering of courses: 과목 제공
    - be bound to do: ~할 승산이 크다 (= be likely to do)

4. 그리고 성적 제출 후에는 학점에 만족하지 않는 학생들의 전화와 e메일에 시달리게 된다.

>>> Furthermore, the professors, soon after awarding the grades to the students, are highly likely to get irritated by the calls and emails from those who are not happy with what they get.

- award/ give the grades to: ~에게 학점을 주다

- be highly likely to do: ~할 확률이 높다

- get irritated by: ~때문에 짜증이 나다 (= be besieged/ annoyed/ plagued/ bothered by)

- be happy with: ~에 만족하다, 기뻐하다

5. 현실이 이렇다 보니 교수가 학점을 짜게 주어야 할 이유가 눈곱만큼도 없다.

>>> Given the circumstances, there is no reason whatsoever to give the bad grades to any of the students.

- given/ under the circumstances: 사정이 그러하므로

- there is no reason whatsoever to do: ~할 이유가 전혀 없다

   - whatsoever: (부정문에서 쓰며 부정의 뜻을 강조함)

6. 더 나아가 학생의 취업까지 생각하면 교수의 학점 퍼주기는 쉽게 합리화되어 버린다.

>>> (a) The professors thus feel fully justified in being generous with their grades, especially when they have their students in mind for employment.

- feel justified in doing: ~하는 것을 정당하다고 생각하다

- be generous with: ~을 주는 데 너그럽다

- have someone in mind for: ~에 대해서 아무개를 염두에 두다

(b) The way professors give inflated grades to their students is warranted, especially when they have to think about helping them land their jobs.

- be warranted: ~이 정당화되다
- help someone do: 아무개가 ~하는 것을 돕다

관련 유용 표현

1. 그 대학은 시험중 부정 행위에 대처하기 위해 과감한 조치를 취하면서 누구도 부정행위를 하다 발각되면 퇴학처분을 하기로 결정하였다. 그렇게 될 경우 학교에서 퇴학 기록이 있는 학생은 취업에 큰 어려움을 겪을 가능성이 높다.

- 부정행위에 대처하다: deal with cheating in school exams
    - cheating: 부정 행위
- ~을 위해 과감한 조치를 취하다: take drastic measures to do
    - take measures to do: ~을 하기 위해 조치를 취하다
- 부정행위를 하다 적발되다: be caught in the act of cheating
    - be caught in the act of doing: ~을 하다 붙잡히다
- 학생을 퇴학 처분하기로 결정하다: decided to get a student kicked out of school
- kick someone out of: 아무개를 ~에서 쫓아내다 (= expel someone from)
- 그렇게 될 경우: , in which case
- 학교에서 퇴학 당한 경험이 있는 학생: a student with a history of expulsion from school; a student who was expelled from school

• with a history of: ~의 전례, 경험이 있는
• 취업에 어려움을 겪을 가능성이 크다: be likely to face difficulty in seeking employment
• face/ have difficulty in doing: ~하는 데 어려움을 겪다
• seek employment: 직업을 구하다 (= look for a job)

>>> Taking drastic measures to deal with cheating in school exams, the university has decided to get anyone caught in the act of cheating kicked out of the school, in which case the student with a history of expulsion from the school is likely to face difficulty in seeking employment.

2. 정치인들은 일단 당선만 되면 자기가 내건 공약을 지키지 않아도 시민들이 일일이 따지고 들지 않기 때문에, 그들은 지키지 않을 약속을 마구 떠들지 않을 이유가 눈곱만큼도 없다.

• 정치인들은 일단 당선만 되면: once politicians are elected,
• 시민들이 지키지 않은 선거공약을 일일이 따지고 들지 않는다: Constituents overlook the empty campaign promises/ words.
• 정치인들이 지키지 않을 약속을 마구 떠들다: Politicians make all kinds of big promises that they have no intention of fulfilling
• ~하지 않기 때문에/ 아무개가 ~을 하지 않을 것을 아는데: because they know that someone will not
• ~을 하지 않을 이유가 전혀 없다: it's not surprising at all that

>>> It's not surprising at all that politicians often make all kinds of big campaign promises that they have no intention of fulfilling because they know that their constituents will eventually overlook their empty words once they are elected.

Part 5

건강

38

건강 운동

번역과 영작

나는 최근 몇 년 동안 적어도 일주일에 두 번 30분씩 운동을 해 왔는데 덕분에 건강과 몸매를 나름대로 잘 유지해 왔다. 나는 운동을 통해 나 자신이 얻은 축복에 감사한다. 그 축복이란 맑은 정신, 수면 습관의 개선, 성취감, 날씬한 몸매 등이다. 그전에는 1시간씩 운동한다는 것은 생각지도 못했고 몸매를 위해서는 특단의 조치로 단식을 해야만 했다.

(월간 가정 건강 239호, 2012.03.)

＊ ＊ ＊

Thanks to a 30-minute workout which I've been doing so religiously at least twice a week over the past several years, I've been able to stay fit, keeping my figure in my own way.

I'm so grateful for all the tangible benefits of the exercise, which I am enjoying now, including clear-headedness, improved sleeping habits, a sense of achievement, my slender figure, etc.

I never thought I could ever do an hour of a daily exercise before, when all I ever did was to fast as a unique way of staying in shape.

 B 해설

1. 최근 몇 년 동안 적어도 일주일에 두 번 30분씩 운동을 해 왔는데 덕분에 건강과 몸매를 나름대로 잘 유지해 왔다.

>>> Thanks to a 30-minute workout which I've been doing so religiously at least twice a week over the past several years, I've been able to stay fit, keeping my figure in my own way.

- **thanks to:** ~덕분에 (because of)

- **do a workout/ exercise religiously:** (건강을 위한) 독실하게/ 충실하게 운동을 하다

- **do religiously:** 독실하게 ~을 하다

- **twice a week:** 일주일에 두 번 (= two times a week)

- **over the past several years:** 최근 몇 년 동안

- **stay fit:** 건강하다 (= be in good health; stay/ keep in shape; be in the pink; be/ keep fit)

- **keep one's figure:** 몸매를 유지하다 (= have a good figure)

- **in one's (own) way:** 나름대로, 자기 방식으로

2. 운동을 통해 나 자신이 얻은 축복에 감사한다. 그 축복이란 맑은 정신, 수면 습관의 개선, 성취감, 날씬한 몸매 등이다.

>>> I'm so grateful for all the tangible benefits of the exercise, which I am enjoying now, including clear-headedness, improved sleeping habits, a sense of achievement, my slender figure, etc.

- be grateful/ thankful for: ~에 대해 감사하게 생각하다
- enjoy the benefits of: ~의 혜택을 누리다
    - the benefits/ results of: ~의 혜택
- clear headedness: 맑은 정신
- improved sleeping habits/ sleep pattern: 개선된 수면 습관
- a sense of achievement: 성취감
    - a sense of: ~의 감
- slender figure: 날씬한 몸매

3. 그 전에는 1시간씩 운동한다는 것은 생각지도 못했고 몸매를 위해서는 특단의 조치로 단식을 해야만 했다.

>>> I never thought I could ever do an hour of a daily exercise before, when all I ever did was to fast as a unique way of staying in shape.

- I never thought I could ever do: ~한다는 것은 상상조차 할 수 없었다 (= I never could have imagined doing)
- a daily exercise: 매일 매일 하는 운동 (= a regular exercise on a daily basis)
- all I ever did was (to) do: 내가 한 거라곤 ~하는 것이었다

- **fast**: 단식하다 (= skip meals; go on a diet) **break one's fast**: 단식을 중단하다
- **as a unique way of doing**: ~을 하기 위한 특별한 방법으로
    - **as a way of**: ~의 방법으로
- **stay in shape**: 좋은 몸매를 유지하다

C 관련 유용 표현

1. 나에게 이처럼 꿈에 그리던 직업이 주어지리라곤 상상조차 할 수 없었다. 이 순간 나는 내가 좋은 교육을 받을 수 있도록 모든 정성을 쏟은 내 부모님에게 다시 한 번 감사함을 느낀다. 그러므로 나는 그 분들의 개인적 크나큰 희생이 없었다면 지금의 나는 있을 수 없음을 기억하는 것이 도리라고 굳게 믿는다.

- 꿈에 그리던 직업이 주어지리라곤 상상조차 할 수 없었다: I never could have imagined being offered my dream job.
    - never could have imagined: ~은 상상조차 할 수 없었다
    - offer me my dream job: 나에게 꿈에 그리던 직업을 제의하다
    - offer a job to someone: 아무개에게 직업을 제의하다
- 이 순간: at the moment
- 내가 좋은 교육을 받을 수 있도록 가능한 모든 정성을 쏟다: pull out all the stops to help me get well educated
    - pull out all stops to do: ~을 하기 위해 모든 노력을 쏘다, 할 수 있는 모든 것을 다 하다
    (= make every effort to do)

- 나는 ~을 굳게 믿는다: I firmly believe that

- 아무개에게 ~을 하는 것이 도리이다: owe it to someone to do

- 오늘날의 내가 되지 못했을 것이다: wouldn't be where I am now

- ~의 희생이 없이는: without one's sacrifice

>>> I never could have imagined being offered my dream job like this. At this moment, once again, I'm so grateful to my parents, who pulled out all the stops to help me get well educated. I, therefore, believe that I owe it to them to remember that I wouldn't be where I am now without their great personal sacrifice.

2. 지난 1년 간 일주일에 세 번 하는 수영 덕에 고질병인 내 허리 통증이 생각지도 않게 말끔하게 나았다.

- 지난 1년간 일주일에 세 번: 3 times a week over the past year

- 수영 덕에: thanks to swimming

- 고질병인 내 허리 통증: my chronic back pain

- 허리 통증이 말끔하게 나았다: my chronic back pain has completely disappeared.

- 병이 나았다: Pain has disappeared; Pain has gone/ stopped/ been relieved

  cf I'm on the mend now: 나는 지금 회복중이다 (= I'm getting better; I'm making a recovery; I'm recuperating (from))

>>> After swimming three times a week over the past year, my chronic back pain has somehow unexpectedly completely disappeared.

39

스트레스와 감기

A
번역과 영작

직장에서 갈등이나 부부관계로 만성 스트레스를 겪는 사람들은 감기에 더 잘 걸리고 감기에 일단 걸리면 그 증상이 더욱 악화된다는 연구 결과가 나왔다. 만성 스트레스 증상이 있는 사람들은 그렇지 않은 사람들에 대면 스트레스 호르몬인 코르티솔(cortisol)이 신체의 염증 반응에 대처를 못하게 함으로써 감기로 인한 고통을 더 키운다는 것이다.

(코메디닷컴뉴스 2012.04.04.)

* * *

A recent study finds that people who are under chronic stress caused by coming into conflict with their co-workers in the workplace or by their troubled marital relationship are more susceptible to a common cold, and that, once they have come down with the illness, the symptoms get even worse.

Compared with stress-free people, those who show the symptoms of chronic stress are likely to suffer more severely from a cold because cortisol, a stress hormone, has proved ineffective against the reaction of the bodily inflammation.

해설

1. 직장에서 갈등이나 부부관계로 만성 스트레스를 겪는 사람들은 감기에 더 잘 걸리고 감기에 일단 걸리면 그 증상이 더욱 악화된다는 연구 결과가 나왔다.

>>> A recent study finds that people who are under chronic stress caused by coming into conflict with their co-workers in the workplace or by their troubled marital relationship are more susceptible to a common cold, and that, once they have come down with the illness, the symptoms get even worse.

• **a study finds that:** ~한 연구 결과가 나오다, 연구에 의하면 ~하다 (= a study shows/ indicates/ reveals that)
  cf 조사 (통계, 연구)에 의하면: an examination (statistics, research) shows/ indicates/ reveals/ suggests that
• **people (who are) under stress:** 스트레스를 겪는 사람 (= people who experience stress)
  • **chronic stress:** 만성 스트레스 **cf** chronic alcoholic: 만성 알코올 중독자

- **stress caused by**: ~때문에 생긴 스트레스 (= stress created/ caused by)

- **come into conflict with their co-workers in the workplace**: 직장 동료와의 갈등을 겪다 (= be in trouble with their co-workers)

  - **co-workers**: 직장 동료

  - **in the workplace**: 직장 내

- **troubled marital relationship**: 결혼 생활의 문제 (= problems with marital relationship)

- **be susceptible to a common cold**: 감기에 걸리기 쉽다 (= be likely to get/ catch a cold)

  [cf] **get/ catch a cold; come down with a cold**: 감기에 걸리다
  develop/ suffer from Alzheimer's: 알츠하이머병에 걸리다
  be struck by AIDS; contract AIDS: 에이즈에 걸리다

- **once they have come down with a cold**: 감기에 일단 걸리면

  - **once**: 일단 ~하면 → 접속사

  - **come down with**: (병에) 걸리다

  [cf] **I feel a little under the weather today**: 나는 오늘 몸 상태가 좋지 않다.

- **the symptoms get worse**: 증상이 악화되다 (= the symptoms worsen/ deteriorate)

2. 만성 스트레스 증상이 있는 사람들은 그렇지 않은 사람들에 대면 스트레스 호르몬인 코르티솔(cortisol)이 신체의 염증 반응에 대처를 못하게 함으로써 감기로 인한 고통을 더 키운다는 것이다.

>>> Compared with stress-free people, those who show the symptoms of chronic stress are likely to suffer more severely from a cold because cortisol, a stress hormone, has proved ineffective against the reaction of the bodily inflammation.

- **compared with/ to**: ~과 비교하면
- **those who show the symptoms of the chronic stress**: 만성 스트레스 증상이 있는 사람
    - **those who**: ~하는 사람
    - **show the symptoms**: ~의 증상이 있다 (= suffer/ suffer from the symptoms)
- **be likely to suffer more severely from a cold**: 감기를 더 심하게 앓기 쉽다
- **a stress hormone has proved/ proven ineffective against the reaction**: 스트레스 호르몬이 신체의 염증 반응에 효력이 없다
    - **prove ineffective against**: ~에 효력이 없다
    - **the reaction of**: ~의 반응
    - **the bodily inflammation**: 신체의 염증

 관련 유용 표현

1. 중국 정부가 한 자녀 갖기 정책을 완화하면서 자녀가 하나뿐인 많은 중국 젊은 부부들은 조만간 자녀를 한 명 더 갖게 되어 몹시 흥분해 있다.

- 한 자녀 갖기 정책을 완화하다: relax its grip on the one-child policy
    - relax its grip on: ~의 통제력을 완화하다
- 자녀가 하나뿐인 부부들: couples with only one child
- 조만간: sooner or later
- 또 하나의 자녀를 갖게 되다: have another child on the way
- ~하게 되어 몹시 흥분하다: be thrilled to do; be excited to do

>>> With the Chinese government set to relax its grip on the one-child policy, many young Chinese couples with only child would be thrilled to see sooner or later another on the way.

2. 병원의 중환자실에서 수퍼박테리아 감염사례가 자주 있다. 일단 수퍼박테리아에 감염되면 어떤 항생제도 듣지 않는다는 점이 공포스럽다.

- 병원의 중환자실: intensive care unit in the hospitals
- 수퍼박테리아에 감염사례가 자주 있다: patients often get infected with superbugs
- 항생제가 수퍼박테리아에 듣지 않는다: Antibiotics are prevented by superbugs from curing the infections; Antibiotics have proved ineffective against superbugs; Antibiotics don't work against superbugs; Superbugs are resistant to antibiotics
- 공포스럽다: a cause for concern; cause concern; arouse concern

>>> Patients in the intensive care units in the hospitals often get infected with superbugs, which is a cause for concern because they prevent antibiotics from curing the infections.

40

직업성 암

직업성 암으로 연간 6,000명 가까운 사망자가 발생한다는 조사 결과가 나왔다. 직업성 암은 산업 현장에서 일하는 동안 발암물질에 지속적으로 노출되면서 생기는 암이다. 현장 근로자들의 발암물질 노출이 심각한 수준임을 새삼 일깨워준다. 작업장 흡연 문제도 심각하다. 발암물질과 접촉하면서 흡연할 경우 암 발생률이 훨씬 높아진다는 사실은 이미 의학적인 상식이다. 정부와 기업은 대대적인 금연운동도 함께 펼쳐야 마땅하다.

(중앙일보 오피니언 사설 2012.07.03.)

＊ ＊ ＊

The recent survey finds that nearly as many as 6,000 people die each year from occupationally-related cancer, which is caused by their prolonged exposure to cancer-causing substances found in the industrial zones.

Once again, we are made aware of workers' massive exposure to the cancer-causing substances in their workplace.

Smoking in the workplace also poses serious problems. It's medically a well-known fact that people who smoke while coming into contact with cancer-causing substances are at higher risk of developing cancer.

It is, therefore, imperative for the government, together with the businesses, to run a major anti-smoking campaign across Korea.

 해설

1. 직업성 암으로 연간 6,000명 가까운 사망자가 발생한다는 조사 결과가 나왔다. 직업성 암은 산업 현장에서 일하는 동안 발암물질에 지속적으로 노출되면서 생기는 암이다.

>>> The recent survey finds that nearly as many as 6,000 people die each year from occupationally-related cancer, which is caused by their prolonged exposure to cancer-causing substances found in the industrial zones.

• occupationally-related cancer: 직업성 암
• be caused by: ~이 원인이 되다
• exposure to: ~에의 노출
• cancer-causing substances: 발암 물질
• industrial zone: 산업 현장, 단지

2. 현장 근로자들의 발암물질 노출이 심각한 수준임을 새삼 일깨워준다.

>>> (a) Once again, we are made aware of workers' massive exposure to the cancer-causing substances in their workplace.

- **once again**: 다시 한 번 (= once more)
- **be made aware of**: ~을 깨우다 (= bring something to our attention; be awakened to; be reminded of)
- **massive exposure to**: ~에 대한 과다 노출
- **in their workplace**: 일터에서

>>> (b) This is another reminder that the workers are constantly exposed to the excessive level of the cancer-causing substances in their workplace.

- **this is a reminder that**: 이것이 ~을 생각나게 하다
- **be exposed to**: ~에 노출되다

>>> (c) Once again, we are awakened to the fact that the workers suffer a high level of the cancer-causing substances found in their workplace.

- **suffer**: (좋지 않은 것에) 시달리다

3. 작업장 흡연 문제도 심각하다. 발암물질과 접촉하면서 흡연할 경우 암 발생률이 훨씬 높아진 다는 사실은 이미 의학적인 상식이다.

>>> Smoking in the workplace also poses serious problems. It's medically a well-known fact that people who smoke while coming into contact with cancer-causing substances are at higher risk of developing cancer.

- **pose problems**: 문제를 야기하다 (= present/ cause/ create problems)
- **it is a well-known fact that**: ~은 잘 알려진 사실이다 (= it is common knowledge that)
- **come into contact with**: ~과 접촉하다
- **be at (higher) risk of doing**: ~할 위험성이 (더) 높다

4. 정부와 기업은 대대적인 금연운동도 함께 펼쳐야 마땅하다.

>>> It is, therefore, imperative for the government, together with the businesses, to run a major anti-smoking campaign across Korea.

- **it is imperative for A to do B**: A는 B를 반드시 해야 한다
- **run a major anti-smoking campaign**: 대대적인 금연 운동을 하다
  - **run a campaign**: 캠페인을 벌이다

1. 담배를 피우는 사람들은 흡연이 폐암과 관련이 있다는 사실을 알면서도 담배 끊기를 힘들어한다.

   • 담배를 피우다: smoke (= light a cigarette; light up)

   • 흡연이 폐암과 관련이 있다: Smoking causes lung cancer. (= Lung cancer is linked to smoking.)

   • ~을 잘 알다: be fully/ perfectly aware that; know full well/ only too well/ perfectly well that

   • 담배를 끊다: kick the habit; break the habit; stop smoking

   • ~하기가 힘들다: find it hard to do

   >>> **Those who smoke find it hard to kick the habit, although they are fully aware that smoking causes lung cancer.**

2. 어떤 기업의 작업장 근로자들이 여러 명 백혈병으로 사망하면서 그 원인이 직업과 관련이 있음을 규명하는데 오랜 세월이 걸렸다.

   • 작업장 근로자: workers in the workplace

   • 어떤 기업의 근로자: workers with/ employed by a company; working for a company

   • 백혈병으로 사망하다: die of leukemia

   • ~의 원인을 규명하다: determine the cause of

   • ~관 관련이 있다: be related/ linked to

   • 오랜 세월이 걸리다: it takes years to do

>>> After many workers with a Korean company died of leukemia in suspicious circumstances, it took years to determine the cause of the cancer, which eventually turned out to be closely linked to their work in the workplace.

분노의 우울증 유발

41

A 번역과 영작

화를 내는 건 인간이 가진 자연스러운 감정이다. 화날 때마다 그때그때 풀어서 우울증에 걸리지 않도록 하고, 만약 걸렸으면 감기 치료하듯이 꼭 치료를 해야만 낫는단다. 우리나라는 경제협력개발기구 국가 중 자살률 1위, 전 세계에서는 2위다. 사는 것보다 죽는 게 편하다고 생각하는 사람이 세계에서 둘째로 많다는 말이다. 자살의 가장 큰 원인은 우울증이고 환자 중 노인이 젊은 사람의 다섯 배라고 한다.

(중앙일보 오피니언 2012.08.06.)

* * *

Getting angry is part of the process of expressing natural human feelings.

Therefore, whenever you lose your temper, you would be better off releasing your anger immediately to prevent depression from developing.

If you are already suffering from the mental illness, in order to make a full recovery, you are highly recommended to seek medical attention as you would when you get a common cold treated.

Korea has the highest suicide rate among the member countries of the OECD, ranking second in the world, that is, in terms of the number of the people who feel that they would rather die than struggle for survival.

In Korea, depression is reported to be the key contributing factor in suicide with the old patients being five times more susceptible to the mental disorder than the younger ones.

 해설

1. 화를 내는 건 인간이 가진 자연스러운 감정이다.

> >> Getting angry is part of the process of expressing natural human feelings.

- **get angry:** 화를 내다 (= get mad; lose one's temper)
- **part of the process of:** ~의 과정의 일부
- **the process of doing:** ~하는 과정
- **express/ show feelings:** 감정을 나타내다

2. 화날 때마다 그때그때 풀어서 우울증에 걸리지 않도록 하고, 만약 걸렸으면 감기 치료하듯이 꼭 치료받을 것을 가장 권한다.

>>> Therefore, whenever you lose your temper, you would be better off releasing your anger immediately to prevent depression from developing. If you are already suffering from the mental illness, in order to make a full recovery, you are highly recommended to seek medical attention as you would when you get a common cold treated.

- **lose one's temper**: 화를 내다 (= get angry)
- **be better off doing**: ~을 하는 것이 좋다
- **release one's anger**: 화를 풀다 (= do not hold back one's anger; vent your anger)
  cf get it out of your system: 화를 풀기 위해 ~을 하다
- **prevent A from doing B**: A가 B를 못하도록 예방하다
- **depression develops**: 우울증이 발생하다
- **if you are already suffering from mental illness**: 정신적인 병을 이미 앓고 있다면
- **make a full recovery**: 완전히 회복하다 (= recover fully)
- **you are highly recommended to do**: 사람들이 ~을 할 것을 권고하는 바이다 (= you would be well advised to do)
- **seek medical attention**: 치료를 받다 (= get medical treatment; see your doctor)
- **as you would when you get a common cold treated**: 감기를 치료하듯이
  - **a common cold**: 감기

3. 우리나라는 경제협력개발기구 국가 중 자살률 1위, 전 세계에서는 2위다. 사는 것보다 죽는 게 편하다고 생각하는 사람이 세계에서 둘째로 많다는 말이다.

>>> Korea has the highest suicide rate among the member countries of the OECD, ranking second in the world, that is, in terms of the number of the people who feel that they would rather die than struggle for survival.

- have the highest rate: 비율이 제일 높다

- the member countries of the OECD: 경제협력개발기구 국가들

- rank second: 2위다 (= be placed 2nd)

- that is (to say): 즉, 다시 말해

- in terms of: ~의 면에서, ~으로 말하면

- the number of the people who do: ~하는 사람 수

- would rather do than something: 무엇을 하기 보다 차라리 ~하고 싶다 (= prefer to do)

- struggle/ fight for survival: 살기 위해 바둥거리다

4. 자살의 가장 큰 원인은 우울증이고 환자 중 노인이 젊은 사람의 다섯 배라고 한다.

>>> In Korea, depression is reported to be the key contributing factor in suicide with the old patients being five times more susceptible to the mental disorder than the younger ones.

- be reported to be: ~으로 보도되다/ 알려지다

- the key/ contributing factor in: ~의 주요 원인

- with the old patients being five times more susceptible to the mental disorder than the younger ones: 노인 환자가 젊은 환자보다 정신 질환에 걸릴 확률이 다섯 배나 되면서

  - be susceptible to: (질병 등에) 걸리기 쉽다 (= be likely to suffer from; be at risk from; be prone to)

  - a mental disorder: 정신 장애

관련 유용 표현

1. 한국은 OECD 회원국 중 자살률이 가장 높고 자살 성향이 있는 사람 수로는 세계 2위다.

- OECD 회원국 중 자살률이 가장 높은 한국은: Korea, with the suicide rate highest among the OECD member countries, is
- in terms of: ~로 말하면, ~으로 보면
- people with suicidal tendencies: 자살 성향이 있는 사람
- 세계 2위다: (be) ranked 2nd in the world

>>> Korea, with the suicide rate highest among the OECD member countries, is second in the world in terms of the number of people with suicidal tendencies.

2. 우리 나라 65세 이상 노인 평균 빈곤율이 49.6%로 OECD 국 중 1위이다. 즉 100명 중에 거의 50명이 빈곤에 시달린다는 뜻이다.

- 65세 이상 노인: the old people over (the age of) 65
- 노인 빈곤율: the poverty rate for the elderly
- 49.6%의 노인: 49.6% of the elderly
- OECD 국 중 1위다: be ranked number one among the OECD member countries
- 빈곤에 시달리다: be mired in poverty; live below the poverty line; live in grinding poverty; be caught in the poverty trap

>>> In terms of the poverty rate for the elderly, Korea, with 49.6% of the old people over 65 living in poverty, is ranked number one among the OECD member countries; in other words, nearly 50 Koreans out of 100 in that category are mired in poverty.

42

금연 운동

A

번역과 영작

블룸버그 뉴욕시장이 10년 전부터 대대적인 금연운동을 벌이고 있지만 한국과 중국 등 아시아계의 비협조로 한계를 드러내고 있다. 뉴욕타임스는 2002~2010년 뉴욕에 거주하는 다른 인종들의 흡연율은 대부분 줄었지만 유독 아시아계의 흡연율은 요지부동이었다고 전했다. 세계보건기구는 통계에서 한국과 중국 남성의 70%가 담배를 피우는 것으로 돼 있다면서, 이런 현상이 일정 부분 본국에 뿌리를 두고 있다고 밝혔다. 뉴욕의과대학의 조교수는 "흡연에 관한 한 아시아계에는 뉴욕시의 금연정책과 프로그램이 잘 침투되지 않는 집요한 문화적 규범이 있다"고 지적했다. 아시아계 사이에는 서로에게 담배나 술을 선물하는 문화가 일상화돼 있다는 것이다.

(한국일보 2012.03.03.)

* * *

A major anti-smoking campaign spearheaded by Mayor of New York

Bloomberg over the past 10 years now suffers a setback because of lack of support from Asians, including Koreans and Chinese.

The New York Times has reported that Asians are the only ones who persist in their refusal to quit smoking, while the smoking rate in general significantly dropped among the non-Asians who lived in New York from 2002 to 2010.

According to the official statistics released by WHO, 70% of Koreans and Chinese men smoke, with their smoking habit somewhat ingrained in their respective homelands.

In the meantime, an assistant professor at a medical school in New York indicated that, where smoking is concerned, Asians fully conform to their accepted cultural norms, which are unaffected by the New York's no-smoking policy and its related programs.

He added that culturally it is customary for Asians to occasionally exchange as a gift a carton of cigarettes or a bottle of wine.

해설

1. 블룸버그 뉴욕시장이 10년 전부터 대대적인 금연운동을 벌이고 있지만 한국과 중국 등 아시아계의 비협조로 한계를 드러내고 있다.

>>> A major anti-smoking campaign spearheaded by Mayor of New York Bloomberg over the past 10 years now suffers a setback because of lack of support from Asians, including Koreans and Chinese.

- a major anti-smoking campaign spearheaded/ led by Mayor: 시장이 이끄는 대대적인 금연운동
- over the past 10 years: 과거 10년 간
- suffer a setback: 중대한 차질을 겪다 (= hit a snag; run into a snag; get nowhere; remain deadlocked; be at an impasse)
- support from: ~로 부터의 지원

2. 뉴욕타임스는 2002~2010년 뉴욕에 거주하는 다른 인종들의 흡연율은 대부분 줄었지만 유독 아시아계의 흡연율은 요지부동이었다고 전했다.

>>> The New York Times has reported that Asians are the only ones who persist in their refusal to quit smoking, while the smoking rate in general significantly dropped among the non-Asians who lived in New York from 2002 to 2010.

- the only ones who persist in their refusal to quit smoking: 끈질기게 금연을 거절하는 유일한 사람들 (= the only ones who adamantly refuse to quit smoking)

- persist in one's refusal to do: 끈질기게 ~하길 거절하다
- refusal to do: ~하는 것에 대한 거절
- quit/ give up smoking: 금연
- significantly dropped: 상당히 줄었다 (= declined; fell; went down)

3. 세계보건기구는 통계에 한국과 중국의 남성 70%가 담배를 피우는 것으로 돼 있다면서, 이런 현상이 일정 부분 본국에 뿌리를 두고 있다고 밝혔다.

>>> According to the official statistics released by WHO, 70% of Koreans and Chinese men smoke, with their smoking habit somewhat ingrained in their respective homelands.

- according to the official statistics: 공식 통계에 따르면 (= based on the official statistics)
- the official statistics released by WHO: 세계 보건기구가 내놓은 공식 통계
- be released by: ~에 의해 발표되다 (= be issued; reported by)
- , with something ingrained in: 뭔가가 ~에 뿌리를 두고 있는 상황에서
  - be ingrained in: (습관 등이) 뿌리를 내리다 (= be developed/ formed in; originated in; entrenched; take root in)
- their respective homelands: 그들 각자의 출신국

4. 뉴욕의과대학의 조교수는 "흡연에 관한 한 아시아계에는 뉴욕시의 금연정책과 프로그램이 잘 침투되지 않는 집요한 문화적 규범이 있다"고 지적했다.

>>> In the meantime, an assistant professor at a medical schoolin New York indicated that, where smoking is concerned, Asians fully conform to their accepted cultural norms, which are unaffected by the New York's no-smoking policy and its related programs.

- in the meantime: 한편 (= meanwhile)
- where smoking is concerned: 흡연에 관한 한 (= as far as smoking is concerned; when it comes to smoking)
- conform to their cultural norms: 그들의 문화적 규범에 따르다
    - conform to: (규칙, 규범 등을) 지키다, 따르다 (= adhere to; stick to; cling to; comply with)
- , which are unaffected by: (앞 내용이) ~에 영향을 받지 않는다

5. 아시아계 사이에는 서로에게 담배나 술을 선물하는 문화가 일상화돼 있다는 것이다.

>>> He added that culturally it is customary for Asians to occasionally exchange as a gift a carton of cigarettes or a bottle of wine.

- add that: ~이라고 덧붙이다
- it is customary for someone to do: 아무개가 ~을 하는 것은 관례다
- as a gift: 선물로
- a carton of cigarette: 담배 한 보루
- a bottle of wine: 술 한 병

1. 한국에서는 명절인 음력 8월 15일 추석날 사람들이 조상의 묘를 찾아가 그 앞에서 경의의 표시로 엎드려 절을 하고, 반드시 송편을 먹어야 하는 것이 풍속이다.

- 음력 8월 15일: August 15th of the lunar calendar
- 명절, 국경일: a national holiday
- 조상의 묘 앞에서: in front of the ancestral graves
- 엎드려 절을 하다: bow down
- 경의의 표시로: as a mark of respect
- 추석이면 송편을 빼놓지 않고 먹는다: enjoy Korean rice cake, without which the Korean version of Thanksgiving Day would not be complete
- ~을 하는 것은 관습적이다: it is customary that

>>> It is customary that on August 15th of the lunar calendar, traditionally a national holiday in Korea, people visit their ancestral graves and bow down in front of the graves as a mark of respect for their ancestors, then enjoy Songpyon, Korean rice cakes, without which the Korean version of Thanksgiving Day would not be complete.

2. 청년 실업률은 요지부동이고 비정규직은 계속 늘어만 간다. 대기업의 일자리 창출계획도 청년들의 피부에 와닿지 못하는 것 같다.

- 청년 실업률: the youth unemployment rate
- 요지부동이다: remain unchanged
- 비정규직은 계속 늘어나다: keep offering only temporary jobs

- 대기업의 일자리 창출 계획: the corporation's policy on the creation of jobs
- 청년들의 피부에 와 닿지 못하는 것 같다: seems to fall far short of the young job seekers' expectations; doesn't seem to work well to improve the young job seekers'unemployment situation

>>> While the youth unemployment remains unchanged with more companies offering only the temporary jobs, the corporations' policy on the creation of the jobs seems to fall far short of the young job seekers' expectations.

43

자살권 청원

　영국 법원이 전신마비를 앓고 있는 50대 남성이 제기한 '죽을 권리를 인정해 달라'는 소송에 대해 심리를 진행하기로 해 관심을 끌고 있다. 올해 57세인 영국인 토니는 지난 2005년 마비증세가 발생해 목 아래 부분의 신체를 움직일 수 없고 말도 할 수 없게 됐다. 럭비선수 출신으로 회사의 관리자였던 그는 아내와 의료진의 보살핌을 받아야만 살 수 있고 눈을 깜박이는 방법으로 의사 소통을 하고 있다. 그는 "삶에 진저리가 나고 이렇게 살고 싶지 않다" 며 지난 2007년부터 의사들이 권하는 생명 연장과 관련된 일체의 약 복용을 거부하고 있다. 그는 마침내 지난 1월 아내를 통해 지방법원에 자신의 목숨을 끊는 의사가 살인죄로 처벌받지 않도록 법원이 선언해 달라는 소송을 냈다.

(조선닷컴 2012.03.12.)

* * *

Our attention is being drawn to the decision made by a British court to hear the case brought to the court by a man in his 50's, who pleaded for the right to die while suffering from the complete paralysis of the whole body.

Tony, a 57-year-old Briton, has not been able to move his body from the neck down, nor has he ever been able to talk, ever since the symptom of the paralysis developed in 2005.

Therefore, it is only with the personal assistance of his wife and the medical staff that the Briton, a former rugby player, who was once a company director, can sustain his life without being able to communicate except by blinking his eyes.

What is worse, since 2007, he has been obstinately refusing to take the medicine prescribed by his doctors to prolong his life, only saying "I'm sick and tired of my life. So I really don't want to continue to live like this."

Then, last January, he finally had a petition filed with the district court by his wife on his behalf, requesting the court to declare that whichever doctor helps end his life will not face a murder charge.

1. 영국 법원이 전신마비를 앓고 있는 50대 남성이 제기한 '죽을 권리를 인정해 달라'는 소송에 대해 심리를 진행하기로 해 관심을 끌고 있다.

>>> Our attention is being drawn to the decision made by a British court to hear the case brought to the court by a man in his 50's, who pleaded for the right to die while suffering from the complete paralysis of the whole body.

- draw attention to: (사람들의) 주의가 ~에 쏠리다 → ~가 관심을 끌고 있다
- make a decision to do: ~을 하기로 결정하다 (= decide to do)
- bring a case to court: 소송을 제기하다
- a man in his 50's: 50대의 남성
- plead for: ~을 청원하다 (= make a plea for)
- the right to die: 죽을 권리 (= suicide rights; being allowed to die)
- suffer from the complete paralysis of the whole body: 전신이 마비되다

2. 올해 57세인 영국인 토니는 지난 2005년 마비증세가 발생해 목 아래 부분의 신체를 움직일 수 없고 말도 할 수 없게 됐다.

>>> Tony, a 57-year-old Briton, has not been able to move his body from the neck down, nor has he ever been able to talk, ever since the symptom of the paralysis developed in 2005.

- a 57-year-old Briton: 57세의 영국인

- move his body: 몸을 움직이다

- from the neck down: 목부터 그 밑으로

  cf from the president down to the office boy: 대통령에서 사환에 이르기까지 모두

- the symptom of the paralysis: 마비 증세

- the symptoms develop/ occur: 증상이 나타나다

3. 럭비선수 출신으로 회사의 관리자였던 그는 아내와 의료진의 보살핌을 받아야만 살 수 있고 눈을 깜박이는 방법으로 의사 소통을 하고 있다.

>>> Therefore, it is only with the personal assistance of his wife and the medical staff that the Briton, a former rugby player, who was once a company director, can sustain his life without being able to communicate except by blinking his eyes.

- it ---- that: that 이하는 ---- 이다 (→ 강조 구문)

- with the assistance of: ~의 도움으로, 보살핌을 받아 (= with the help/ aid of)

- the medical staff: 의료진

- sustain/ maintain one's life: ~의 생명을 유지하다

- without being able to communicate: 의사소통을 할 수 없이

- except by blinking his eyes: 눈을 깜박이는 방법 외에는

    - blink eyes: 눈을 깜박이다

4. 그는 "삶에 진저리가 나고 이렇게 살고 싶지 않다" 며 지난 2007년부터 의사들이 권하는 생명 연장과 관련된 일체의 약 복용을 거부하고 있다.

>>> What is worse, since 2007, he has been obstinately refusing to take the medicine prescribed by his doctors to prolong his life, only saying "I'm sick and tired of my life. So I really don't want to continue to live like this."

- **what is worse**: 설상가상으로
- **obstinately refuse to do**: ~하길 완강히 거절하다 (= stubbornly/ adamantly refuse to do)
- **take medicine**: 약을 복용하다 (= be on medication)
- **prescribe medicine**: 약을 처방하다
- **prolong life**: 생명을 연장하다
- **be sick and tired of**: ~이 지긋지긋하다 (= be sick to death; be sick to the back teeth of; be fed up with)
- **don't want to continue to live like this**: 이렇게 계속 살고 싶지 않다 (= don't want to live this way; get tired of living this way)

5. 그는 마침내 지난 1월 아내를 통해 지방법원에 자신의 목숨을 끊는 의사가 살인죄로 처벌받지 않도록 법원이 선언해 달라는 소송을 냈다.

>>> Then, last January, he finally had a petition filed with the district court by his wife on his behalf, requesting the court to declare that whichever doctor helps end his life will not face a murder charge.

- **the district court:** 지방 법원

   appellate court: 고등법원, 항소법원 the Supreme Court: 대법원

- **end/ take one's life:** ~의 목숨을 끊다

   physician-assisted suicide: 의사의 도움을 받아 자살하는 행위

- **face a murder charge:** 살인죄를 받아 (= be charged with murder)

관련 유용 표현

1. 영어 글쓰기는 누구에게나 저절로 되는 것이 아니다. 그것은 시간과 연습과 끈기가 필요하다.

- 영어로 글쓰기: writing in English

- 그것은 저절로 되는 것이 아니다: it does not come naturally

  - comes naturally to someone: 아무개에게 ~이 저절로 이루어지다

- 그것은 시간과 연습과 끈기가 필요하다: it takes ~ to do

  - it takes something to do: ~을 하는 데는 무엇이 필요하다

>>> Being able to write in English does not come naturally to anyone learning English. It takes time, practice and patience to improve this skill.

2. 올해 아카데미 시상식에는 모두 뛰어난 작품이 후보로 올라와서 과연 어느 영화가 최우수작품상을 받을지 관심을 끌고 있다.

- 뛰어난 작품이 후보로 오르다: great movies are nominated as strong candidates for the coveted prize
- 최우수 작품상을 받다: win the coveted prize; win the prize for the best picture
- 어느 영화가 최우수 작품상을 받을지 관심을 끌다: draw our attention to which of those is most likely to win the coveted prize; Our attention is drawn to the likely winner; We are curious to find out which of these movies will win the coveted prize.

>>> This year, with many great movies nominated as strong candidates for the Academy Award, our attention is drawn to which of those is most likely to win the coveted prize.

44

당뇨

당뇨병이란 한마디로 혈당이 지속적으로 높은 상태를 말한다. 인슐린이 없으면 지나치게 많은 당이 혈액에 남아있게 된다. 오랜 시간 동안 잘 조절되지 않은 당뇨병은 혈관과 신경에 손상을 주게 되고 눈, 심장, 콩팥, 다리, 발, 남성의 발기 능력에 영향을 미치는 문제들의 위험성을 높이게 된다.

* * *

Diabetes is simply defined as a serious medical condition in which there is a persistently high level of sugar in the blood.

Without insulin, the presence of excessive sugar would be retained in the blood.

Diabetes, if left uncontrolled for an extended period of time, could cause blood vessel and nerve damage, increasing the risk of developing all kinds of diseases, which affect the eyes, heart, kidneys, legs, feet and erectile function.

 해설

1. 당뇨병이란 한마디로 혈당이 지속적으로 높은 상태를 말한다. 인슐린이 없으면 지나치게 많은 당이 혈액에 남아있게 된다.

>>> Diabetes is simply defined as a serious medical condition in which there is a persistently high level of sugar in the blood. Without insulin, the presence of excessive sugar would be retained in the blood.

- **be defined as:** ~라고 정의하다 (= define A as B)
- **in a serious medical condition:** 심각한 건강상태이다
- **a persistently high level of sugar:** 지속적으로 높은 혈당
- **without insulin, the presence of excessive sugar would be retained in the blood:** 인슐린이 없으면 지나치게 많은 당이 혈당에 남아있다 (= lack of insulin would result in the presence of excessively high sugar content in the blood; if it were not for insulin, too much sugar would be present in the blood)
  - **without insulin:** 인슐린이 없다면 (= if it were not for insulin; but for insulin)
  - **the presence of:** ~이 있음 (= the existence of)
  - **sugar content:** 혈당 함량

2. 오랜 시간 동안 잘 조절되지 않은 당뇨병은 혈관과 신경에 손상을 주게 되고 눈, 심장, 콩팥, 다리, 발, 남성의 발기 능력에 영향을 미치는 문제들의 위험성을 높이게 된다.

>>> Diabetes, if left uncontrolled for an extended period of time, could cause blood vessel and nerve damage, increasing the risk of developing all kinds of diseases, which affect the eyes, heart, kidneys, legs, feet and erectile function.

- **diabetes could cause**: 당뇨병은 ~의 원인이 된다 (= diabetes may cause)

- **if (it is) left uncontrolled**: 조절되지 않으면 (= if (it is) untreated)

- **for an extended period of time**: 장기간 (= for a long period of time)

- **cause blood vessel and nerve damage**: 혈관과 신경에 손상을 주다

    - **cause damage**: 손상을 주다

    - **blood vessel**: 혈관

    - **nerve**: 신경

- **increase the risk of doing**: ~할 위험성을 높이다

- **develop disease**: 병을 유발하다

- **affect the eyes**: 눈에 영향을 주다

- **erectile function**: 발기 기능 **cf** **erectile dysfunction**: 발기 부진

1. 몇 년 전만 해도 치료 받지 않고 얼마 동안 그냥 내버려두면 치명적으로 심각한 병도 요즘은 의술의 발달로 완치될 수 있다.

- 몇 년 전만 해도: only a few years ago
- 치료 받지 않고 내버려두면: if left untreated
- 얼마동안: for an extended period of time
- 치명적으로 심각한 병: a serious life-threatening disease
- 의술의 발달로: thanks to advances in medical technology
- advances in: ~의 발달
- ~이 완치되다: ~is completely cured

>>> Some serious diseases, which could have been life-threatening only a few years ago, if left untreated for an extended period of time, can now be completely cured, thanks to advances in state-of-the-art medical technology.

2. 인플레이션이라 한마디로 물가가 지속적으로 상승하여 화폐가치가 떨어지는 것을 의미한다.

- 인플레이션이란 ~을 의미한다: Inflation is defined as
- 한 마디로: simply
- 물가의 지속적인 상승: a continuing increase in prices
- 화폐가치가 떨어지다: The value of currency/ money declines; Currency is devalued.

>>> Inflation is simply defined as a continuing increase in prices, which causes the value of currency to decline.

Part 6

결혼

45

잘못된 결혼관

　　정신과 전문의들은 "한국 사회가 결혼비용 때문에 집단적으로 마음의 병을 앓고 있다"고 했다. "한국 사회가 집단적으로 결혼의 본질을 잊고 있다, 사랑해서 결혼해야 하는데, 지금 결혼 과정은 사랑을 놓치고 비즈니스가 됐다. 여기서 각종 사회문제가 다 발생한다. 저출산, 섹스리스 부부, 황혼이혼…"

(조선일보 2012.03.24.)

＊ ＊ ＊

　　Psychiatrists claim that Koreans have been collectively going through emotional pain stemming from huge wedding expenses for their kids, that they fail to grasp the true essence of marriage, that, although love should be the basis of all marriages, the current process of marriage, for lack of love, has turned into a business deal, and that, as a result, Korean society as a whole is beset with all kinds of social problems, including a low birthrate, sexless couples and 'gray divorce'…

1. 정신과 전문의들은 "한국 사회가 결혼비용 때문에 집단적으로 마음의 병을 앓고 있다"고 했다.

>>> Psychiatrists claim that Koreans have been collectively going through emotional pain stemming from huge wedding expenses for their kids,...

• go through pain: 고통을 겪다 (= suffer/ experience pain; be in pain)

• stem from: ~에 기인한 (= caused by)

• wedding expenses for their kids: 그들 자녀의 결혼 비용

2. "한국 사회가 집단적으로 결혼의 본질을 잊고 있다, 사랑해서 결혼해야 하는데, 지금 결혼 과정은 사랑을 놓치고 비즈니스가 됐다.

>>> ...... that they fail to grasp the true essence of marriage, that, although love should be the basis of all marriages, the current process of marriage, for lack of love, has turned into a business deal,...

• grasp/ understood the essence of: ~의 본질을 이해하다

• love should be the basis of marriage: 사랑이 결혼의 토대가 되다 (= marriage should be based/ founded on love; marry someone for love)

• for lack of love: 사랑이 결핍되어, 사랑을 놓치고

• turn into: ~으로 변하다 (= be transformed into)

• a business deal: 사업 거래

3. 여기서 각종 사회문제가 다 발생한다. 저출산, 섹스리스 부부, 황혼이혼…"

>>> and that, as a result, Korean society as a whole is beset with all kinds of social problems, including a low birthrate, sexless couples and 'gray divorce'…

- **Korean society as a whole:** 한국 사회 전체
- **be beset with:** (문제 등으로) 꽉 차다 (= be fraught with; be faced with; be confronted with)
- **gray divorce:** 황혼 이혼

관련 유용 표현

1. 사랑이 아닌 경제적인 이유로 결혼하는 부부는 살다가 어느 시점에 결혼이 파탄에 이른다는 소식이 종종 들리는데 이는 별로 놀라운 일도 아니다.

- 사랑이 아닌 경제적인 이유 때문에 결혼하다: get married for economic reasons, not for love
  - not for love: 사랑해서가 아니라
  - for some reasons: 어떤 이유 때문에
- 결혼 생활의 파탄에 직면하다: go through/ face the break-up of a marriage;

• the break-up of marriage: 결혼 파탄 (= marriage break-up; marital break-up)

cf They got divorced. 이혼하다

They split up. 그들은 헤어졌다, 관계가 끝났다

Their marriage broke up. 그들의 결혼 생활이 끝났다.

• ~의 소식을 듣고 놀래다: be surprised to hear that

• at some point in their lives: 인생의 어느 시점에

>>> We are not surprised to hear that today many young couples, who get married for economic reasons, not for love, often go through the break-up of their marriage at some point in their lives.

2. 근래 모든 대학이 교육의 본질을 잊고 너무나 취업 훈련 기관으로 전락하는 게 아닌가 하는 생각이 든다.

• 교육의 본질을 잊다: fail to grasp/ forget the essence of education

• 취업 훈련기관: employment training center

• 전락하다: turn into; be relegated to; be downgraded to; be reduced to

• ~이 아닌가 생각이 든다: I wonder if/ whether; I am not sure whether something is not…

>>> Sometimes I wonder if the universities, failing to grasp the very essence of education in recent times, would turn into employment training centers.

46

국제결혼

A **번역과 영작**

지난 해 한국 남성과 혼인한 외국 여성의 국적은 베트남(34.3%), 중국 (33.9%), 필리핀(9.3%) 등의 순이었으며 한국 여성과 혼인한 외국 남성의 국 적은 중국(24.9%), 일본(22.8%), 미국(21.8%) 등의 순으로 많았다.

(동아일보 2012.04.20.)

* * *

By nationality, the Vietnamese women accounted for 34.3% of all the foreign women who married Korean men last year, followed by the Chinese women with 33.9%, then followed by Philippine women with 9.3%.

Conversely, the Chinese men made up 24.9% of all the interracial marriages involving the foreign men who married Korean women, with the Japanese and American men representing 22.8% and 21.8%, respectively.

1. 지난 해 한국 남성과 혼인한 외국 여성의 국적은 베트남(34.3%), 중국(33.9%), 필리핀(9.3%) 등의 순이었으며 한국 여성과 국제결혼한 외국 남성의 국적은 중국(24.9%), 일본(22.8%), 미국(21.8%) 등의 순으로 많았다.

>>> By nationality, the Vietnamese women accounted for 34.3% of all the foreign women who married Korean men last year, followed by the Chinese women with 33.9%, then followed by Philippine women with 9.3%.
Conversely, the Chinese men made up 24.9% of all the interracial marriages involving the foreign men who married Korean women, with the Japanese and American men representing 22.8% and 21.8%, respectively.

• **by nationality**: 국적으로 보면 **cf** by sex: 성별로 **by age**: 연령 별로

• **account for**: ~에 해당하다 (= represent; constitute; make up; comprise)

• **marry**: 결혼하다 (= tie the knot; get hitched; walk down the aisle; say one's "I do"; exchange vows)

• **, followed by**: 뒤를 이어

• **conversely**: 반대로 (= on the other hand)

• **interracial marriage**: 국제결혼
   cf **arranged marriage**: 중매결혼/ marriage of convenience: 정략결혼

• **involve**: ~을 포함하다

• **respectively**: 각각 (→ 언급한 순서대로)

1. 미국은 다양한 민족집단으로 된 국민들이 같이 살면서 각자 다른 종교적 신념을 가지며 상대방의 의견을 존중하는 다문화 사회로 존재해왔다.

- 다양한 민족집단으로 된 국민: many different ethnic groups of people
- 각자 다른 종교적 신념을 갖는다: share different religious beliefs
- 상대방의 의견을 존중하다: respect other people's views
- 다문화 사회: a multicultural society

>>> The United States of America has always been a multicultural society, where many different ethnic groups of people are living together, sharing their different religious beliefs and respecting other people's views.

2. 2015년 미 Open Doors Report에 따르면 미국내 외국인학생수로 볼 때 한국은 중국과 인도에 이어 3위를 기록하고 있다.

- Open Doors Reports에 따르면: according to *Open Doors Reports*; *Open Doors Reports* say; based on *Open Doors Reports*
- 미국 내 외국인 학생 수로 볼 때: in terms of the number of the foreign students in the U.S.
- 한국은 중국과 인도에 이어 3위를 기록하고 있다: Korea is ranked third behind China and India; China is placed first followed by India, then followed by Korea; Korea is trailing China and India.; Korea is falling/ lagging behind China and India

>>> According to *the 2015 Open Doors Report*, in terms of the number of the foreign students in the U.S., Korea is placed third, after China and India.

47

이혼에 따른 자녀 보호

　대법원은 "미성년 자녀를 둔 협의이혼 당사자들은 자녀 양육 문제에 관해 전문가 상담을 받아야만 이혼 절차를 진행할 수 있도록 할 것"이라고 밝혔다. 이혼이 자녀에게 미치는 영향과 자녀 양육 역할 분담, 자녀의 정서적 안정 등에 관한 상담을 반드시 거치게끔 하겠다는 얘기다.

(중앙일보 사설 2012.10.30.)

＊ ＊ ＊

　The Supreme Court in Korea announced that it would make it mandatory for the married couples with children who file for a no-fault divorce to first receive professional counselling for the childcare issue prior to the start of the divorce proceedings.

　The idea behind such a mandate is to ensure that the couples seeking a divorce go through the process of legal consultation about the impact of the divorce on the children, about the sharing of the responsibility for childcare, and about the children's emotional stability.

 해설

1. 대법원은 "미성년 자녀를 둔 협의이혼 당사자들은 자녀 양육 문제에 관해 전문가 상담을 받아야만 이혼 절차를 진행할 수 있도록 할 것"이라고 밝혔다.

>>> The Supreme Court in Korea announced that it would make it mandatory for the married couples with children who file for a no-fault divorce to first receive professional counselling for the childcare issue prior to the start of the divorce proceedings.

- **the Supreme Court:** 대법원 **cf** **district court:** 지방법원

- **announce that:** ~을 알리다, 밝히다 (= make it clear that; unveil a plan to do)

- **make it mandatory for someone to do:** 아무개가 ~을 하도록 (법으로) 정하다
  (= mandate that someone should do)

- **file for a divorce:** 이혼 소송을 하다 (= petition/ sue for a divorce; go through a divorce) **cf** **file for a bankruptcy:** 파산신청을 하다

- **a no-fault divorce:** 과실을 따지지 않는 협의 이혼

- **professional counselling:** 전문가와의 상담

- **counselling for:** ~을 위한 상담

- **childcare issue:** 양육 문제

- **prior to:** ~전에 (= before)

- **the start of the divorce proceedings:** 이혼 절차의 시작

2. 이혼이 자녀에게 미치는 영향과 자녀 양육 역할 분담, 자녀의 정서적 안정 등에 관한 상담을 반드시 거치게끔 하겠다는 얘기다.

>>> The idea behind such a mandate is to ensure that the couples seeking a divorce go through the process of legal consultation about the impact of the divorce on the children, about the sharing of the responsibility for childcare, and about the children's emotional stability.

- **the idea behind ~ is to do:** 이면의 의도는 ~을 하기 위해서이다

- **a mandate:** 지시

- **seek a divorce:** 이혼을 생각하다

- **go through:** (과정, 절차)를 거치다 (= undergo)

- **legal consultation about:** ~에 관한 법률상담

- **the impact of A on B:** B에 미치는 A의 영향

- **the sharing of the responsibility for:** ~에 관한 책임 분담

- **emotional stability:** 정서적 안정

관련 유용 표현

1. 당신께서 한국에 최대한 편안하고 즐겁게 체류하실 수 있도록 가능한 모든 노력을 다 하겠습니다.

   • 당신의 한국 체류: your stay in Korea

   • 최대로 편안하게 하다: make something as comfortable as possible

   • ~을 하기 위해 모든 노력을 다하다: do my best to do (= pull out all the stops to do; do everything I can to do; give my all to do; make every effort to do)

   >>> We will do my best to make your stay in Korea as comfortable and enjoyable as possible.

2. 좋은 대학에서 학사 학위를 취득해도 좋은 직업을 구할 수 없는 것이 오늘날 고용상황의 실태이다.

   • 좋은 대학에서 학사 학위 취득: a bachelor's degree from a prestigious university

   • 취업이 확실치 않다: be not a path to success in getting a job; do not guarantee a job

   • ~이 현실, 실태이다: the reality is such that; such is the reality that

   • 고용 상황의 현실: the reality of the employment situation

   >>> The reality is that today a degree from a prestigious university is no longer considered to be a path to success in landing a decent job.

48 아시아인의 동족 결혼

A 번역과 영작

미국에서 2010년에 결혼한 아시아 신혼부부 가운데 28%가 타 인종 배우자를 선택했다. 하지만 지난 30년간 아시아 이민자들이 크게 늘면서 자기네 인종 내에서도 배우자를 찾기가 쉬워져 타 인종간 결혼은 감소하는 추세다. 같은 아시아인끼리 결혼하면 언어나 풍습 등이 같아 편리한 점도 작용했다.

(중앙일보 2012.04.01.)

* * *

28% of the newlyweds who tied the knot in America in 2010 chose foreigners as their spouses.

However, with a sharp increase in the number of the Asian immigrants coming to America over the past 30 years, they now find it easier to find their partners from among those who are from the same ethnic background.

As a result, there is a tendency now for the interracial marriage rate to decline among the Asian groups of people.

Feeling more comfortable speaking the same language and sharing the same custom is another reason why the number of the interracial marriages drops in America.

B 해설

1. 미국에서 2010년에 결혼한 아시아 신혼부부 가운데 28%가 타 인종 배우자를 선택했다.

>>> 28% of the newlyweds who tied the knot in America in 2010 chose foreigners as their spouses.

• newlyweds: 신혼 부부
- tie the knot: 결혼하다 (= get married; get hitched)
 cf union, nuptials: 결혼
• choose/ pick A as B: A를 B로 택하다

2. 하지만 지난 30년간 아시아 이민자들이 크게 늘면서 자기네 인종 내에서도 배우자를 찾기가 쉬워져 타 인종간 결혼은 감소하는 추세다.

>>> However, with a sharp increase in the number of the Asian immigrants coming to America over the past 30 years, they now find it easier to find their partners from among those who are from the same ethnic background. As a result, there is a tendency now for the interracial marriage rate to decline among the Asian groups of people.

- with a sharp increase in: ~이 크게 증가하면서
- find it easier to do: ~하는 것이 더 수월하다
- find partners from among those who are: ~한 사람들 중에서 배우자를 찾다
- those who are from the same ethnic background: 같은 소수민족 배경의 사람들
- there is a tendency for someone to do: 아무개가 ~하는 경향이 있다 (= someone tends to do)
- the rate declines: 비율이 감소되다 (= the rate falls/ drops/ goes down)

3. 같은 아시아인끼리 결혼하면 언어나 풍습 등이 같아 편리한 점도 작용했다.

>>> Feeling more comfortable speaking the same language and sharing the same custom is another reason why the number of the interracial marriages drops in America.

- feel comfortable (about/ in) doing: ~하는 것이 마음이 편하다
- share/ follow the same custom: 같은 풍습을 따르다
- be another reason (why): ~을 하는 또 하나의 이유이다
- the number of the interracial marriages drops: 국제결혼이 줄다
- interracial marriage: 국제결혼 (= mixed marriage)
- the number of: ~의 수

관련 유용 표현

1. 안전벨트를 착용하지 않은 사람은 교통사고가 났을 때 착용을 한 사람보다 심한 부상을 당하거나 사망할 확률이 높기 때문에 운전자뿐만 아니라 탑승객도 차 안에서는 안전벨트를 의무적으로 착용해야 한다. 통계에 의하면 안전벨트 착용을 무시한 운전자는 사고로부터 무사하기가 어렵다고 한다.

- 교통사고가 났을 때: in a car accident; in a car crash
- 안전벨트를 착용한 사람: those who buckle up; those who wear/ fasten seat belts
- 부상을 당하다: get injured; get/ suffer an injury
- 안전벨트를 의무적으로 착용하다: it's mandatory to fasten seat belts.
- 안전벨트를 착용하다: fasten/ wear seat belts; buckle one's belt; buckle up; belt up
- 사고가 났을 때 무사할 수 없다: cannot escape unhurt from the car accident

>>> It is mandatory for the passengers as well as the drivers in a car to buckle up because those who don't are more likely to get seriously injured or die in a car accident than those who comply. Statistics show that the drivers who neglect to fasten their seat belts hardly escape unhurt from such a car crash.

2. OPEC가 3년마다 실시하는 국제학업 성취도 평가에서 상하이는 중국과 분리, 단독으로 출전해서 2009년에 이어 2012년에도 1위의 자리를 지켰다.

- 3년 마다: every three years; every third year
- 국제 학업성취도를 실시하다: PISA is held.
  - 국제 학업성취도: The *Programme for International Student Assessment (PISA)*

- 상하이는 중국과 분리, 단독 출전하다: Shanghai participates independently of China in
- 2009년에 이어 2012년에도 1위의 자리를 지키다: be ranked first for the second consecutive time after it was first honored back in 2009; , second consecutive honor, including the one which was first awarded back in 2009

>>> Participating independently of China in PISA, which has been held every third year under auspices of OPEC, Shanghai was ranked first for the second consecutive time after it was first honored back in 2009.

Part 7

기후

49

지구의 온난화

 번역과 영작

지난 100년간 지구의 온도는 평균 0.7도 정도 올랐다. 이 때문에 세계 각국은 기후변화 대책 마련을 위해 골머리를 앓고 있다. 인류뿐 아니라 지구 곳곳의 동식물도 나름대로 기후변화에 대처하느라 분주하다.

(동아일보 2012.01.13.)

* * *

Over the past 100 years, the average temperature of the earth has gone up by 0.7 degree.

As a result, the whole world is now grappling with how to address the problem of the climate change, with the animals and plants as well as the humans on earth hurrying to adapt to the climate change in their own way.

해설

1. 지난 100년간 지구의 온도는 평균 0.7도 정도 올랐다.

>>> Over the past 100 years, the average temperature of the earth has gone up by 0.7 degree.

- **over the past 100 years**: 지난 100년간
- **the temperature has gone up**: 온도가 올랐다 (= the temperature has risen/ soared/ increased)
- **by ~ degree**: ~도로

2. 이 때문에 세계 각국은 기후변화 대책 마련을 위해 골머리를 앓고 있다. 인류뿐 아니라 지구 곳곳의 동식물도 나름대로 기후변화에 대처하느라 분주하다.

>>> As a result, the whole world is now grappling with how to address the problem of the climate change, with the animals and plants as well as the humans on earth hurrying to adapt to the climate change in their own way.

- **as a result**: 그 결과, 그러므로 (= therefore)
- **grapple with**: ~에 고심하다 (= wrestle with; scratch one's head and wonder what to do about; struggle to deal with; be scrambling for solution to; take pains to do)
- **address the problem of**: ~의 문제에 대처하다
- **climate change**: 기후 변화

- **hurry to do:** ~을 하기 위해 서두르다 (= rush to do)

- **in one's own way:** 나름대로

1. 모든 산업국가들은 종의 지속적인 존재를 위협하는 대기오염 문제의 해결에 고심하고 있다. 하지만 문제는 그들 나라의 경제적 생산성을 해치지 않고 효과적인 해결책을 찾기가 쉽지 않다는 것이다.

- 산업국가: an industrialized country
- 지구에서의 종의 지속적인 존재를 위협하다: threaten the continuing existence of the species on the planet
    - the existence of: ~의 존재
    - on the planet: 지구상에 (= on Earth)
- ~의 해결에 고심하다: grapple with how to deal with; try to come up with a solution to the problem of
- 문제는 ~이다: the problem is (that)
- 경제적 생산성을 해치지 않고: without hurting/ affecting the economic productivity
- 효과적인 해결책을 찾기가 쉽지 않다: it's not easy to find any effective solutions to the problem.
    - it's not easy to: ~하기가 쉽지 않다
    - find a solution to: ~의 해결책을 찾다 (= come up with a solution to)

>>> Every industrialized nation is grappling with how to best deal with air pollution, which threatens the continuing existence of the species on the planet. The problem, however, is that it is not easy to find any effective solutions to the problem without hurting the economic productivity of the country.

2. 예산 소진으로 서울시가 어린이집 보육료 지원을 중단하자 자녀를 둔 직장 여성들이 이에 대처하느라 분주하다.

- 예산 소진으로: due to the shortfall in the budget
- 어린이집 보육료 지원: the funding of child care services
- ~을 중단하다: discontinue
- 자녀를 둔 직장 여성: career women with kids
- 대처하느라 분주하다: struggle to cope with their babies

>>> With the funding of childcare service discontinued by the City of Seoul due to the shortfall in the budget, career women with kids are starting to struggle to cope with their babies.

50

태풍

번역과 영작

태풍급 강풍이 전국에 불어 닥쳐 곳곳에서 사고가 발생하고 서울을 비롯한 중부지방에는 19년 만에 '4월의 눈'이 내렸다. 초속 20~30m에 이르는 강풍으로 항공기 120편이 무더기 결항하고, 국내 여객선 운항이 전면 중단됐다.

(조선일보 2012.04.04.)

＊ ＊ ＊

High winds falling into a typhoon category swept through South Korea, creating havoc everywhere, and, in the central part of Korea, including Seoul, snow fell in April for the first time in 19 years.

Gusts of up to 20~30 meters a second forced cancellation of 120 flights, causing massive disruption to domestic ferry services.

해설

1. 태풍급 강풍이 전국에 불어 닥쳐 곳곳에서 사고가 발생하고 서울을 비롯한 중부지방에는 19년 만에 '4월의 눈'이 내렸다.

>>> High winds falling into a typhoon category swept through South Korea, creating havoc everywhere, and, in the central part of Korea, including Seoul, snow fell in April for the first time in 19 years.

- **fall into a typhoon category**: 태풍급에 속하다 (= belong to/ equivalent to/ fit into a typhoon category)
- **High winds sweep through Korea**: 강풍이 한국을 휩쓸다 (= High winds whip/ cut through Korea; High winds bear down on Korea; High winds pummel the Korean peninsula)
- **create havoc**: 폭우, 강풍 등이 피해를 주다 (= play/ wreak/ cause havoc)
- **snow falls/ comes down**: 눈이 내리다
- **for the first time in 19 years**: 19년만에 처음으로

2. 초속 20~30m에 이르는 강풍으로 항공기 120편이 무더기 결항하고, 국내 여객선 운항이 전면 중단됐다.

>>> Gusts of up to 20~30 meters a second forced cancellation of 120 flights, causing massive disruption to domestic ferry services.

- **gusts of up to 20~30 meters a second**: 초속 20~30m에 이르는 강풍 (= max sustained winds of 20 to 30 meters a second)

- **up to:** (시간, 정도, 거리, 양이) ~에 이르는

- **force/ cause cancellation of 120 flights:** 120편의 항공기 운항이 취소되다

- **cause disruption to:** ~을 중단시키다

- **domestic ferry services:** 국내 여객선 운행

관련 유용 표현

1. 나는 이번 주말에 Tom Hanks가 주연을 맡은 영화를 보고 싶지만 불행히도 표가 매진되어서 심야상영 예매권을 누가 취소하지 않는 한 다음 주말까지 기다려야 한다. 그때까지는 꼼짝 못하게 바쁘기 때문이다.

- Tom Hanks가 주연을 맡은 영화: a movie starring Tom Hanks; a movie featuring Tom Hanks as the leading man
- 표가 매진되다: The theater tickets are all sold out.
    - be sold out: 표가 매진되다
- 누가 취소하지 않으면: unless there are any cancellations
    - cancellation: 극장, 기차, 버스 등의 예약 취소
- the midnight showing of the movie: 그 영화의 심야 상영

>>> I really wanted to go to see this Sunday the movie starring Tom Hanks, but unfortunately all the theater tickets are sold out, so unless there are any cancellations for the midnight showing of the movie, I might have to wait until next weekend because I'm all tied up until then.

2. 한국은 수십 년 만에 처음으로 이렇게 따뜻한 12월을 맞고 있다. 눈과 얼음의 나라 러시아도
   79년 만에 가장 따뜻한 겨울을 맞고 있다고 한다.

- 수십 년 만에 처음으로: for the first time in decades
- 한국은 이렇게 따뜻한 12월을 맞고 있다: In Korea the weather now in December is
  unusually warm; Koreans are enjoying the unusually warm weather in December;
  Korea sees the unusually warm December weather.
- 눈과 얼음의 나라: a country of snow and ice
- 러시아도 79년 만에 가장 따뜻한 겨울을 맞고 있다고 한다: the people of Russia are also
  said to be enjoying the warmest weather in winter in 79 years; Russia is also said
  to be spending the warmest weather months in 79 years.; Russians are being
  reported to be passing the warmest winter in 79 years.

>>> In Korea the weather now in December is unusually warm for the
first time in decades. Even in Russia, normally a country of snow and
ice, the people are said to be enjoying the warmest weather in winter
in 79 years.

1. 이근 "정치의 진실" (한국일보 2012.03.29.)

2. "핵 테러" (미주 한국일보 오피니언 2012.03.28.)

3. 김진 "총과 펜과 혀보다 중요한 표" (중앙일보 2012.04.09.)

4. 문창극 "권력의 기질" (중앙일보 2012.07.17.)

5. 김영훈 "세금, 폼나게 냅시다" (중앙일보 2012.07.27.)

6. 이남훈 "21세기 투자DNA 찾아라" (동아일보 2012.02.26.)

7. 안택수 "위대한 청년 실패자를 기다리며" (조선일보 2012.11.27.)

8. "서머 타임 시비" (미주 한국일보 2012.03.14.)

9. "분수 모르는 호화판 아이 기르기가 아이 장래 망친다" (조선닷컴 2012.03.29.)

10. 김혜린 "재정상담 – 여성의 노후준비" (미주 한국일보 2010.07.07.)

11. 이철 "덴마크의 행복 1위 비결" (미주 한국일보 2012.03.28.)

12. "외국 기업 한국 투자 망설이고, 한국 기업은 해외 나가고" (조선일보 사설 2012.04.02.)

13. 배명복 "부자 되는 법, 어렵지 않아요… 안 쓰면 돼요" (중앙일보 2012.06.29.)

14. 송호근 "어느 젊은 택시 기사의 소원" (중앙일보 2012.06.26.)

15. 안상훈 "여성 고용, 새로운 성장 열쇠" (조선일보 2012.03.28.)

16. 박성보 "1등만 기억하는 세상" (중앙 San Francisco)

17. 문용린 "진정한 행복이란 무엇이라 생각하세요?" (월간 마음수련 2012.03.01.)

18. 배명복 "당나귀처럼 사는 한국의 40대는 불혹 아닌 갈매?" (중앙일보 2013.05.07.)

19. 박현정 "어린이 통학차량 운전자, 교통 안전 교육 의무화해야" (동아일보 2012.04.25.)

20. "절전과 요금 현실화로 전력대란 막아야" (중앙일보 2012.06.08.)

21. 박두식 "빨간 신호등과 커닝" (조선닷컴 2012.03.27.)

22. 조해령 "100살을 바라보는 고령화 시대의 삶" (여성중앙 2011.07.27.)

23. 차학봉 "연금 타내려… 아버지 시신 수년간 방치" (조선닷컴 2012.04.04.)

24. "한국 거주 외국인에게 배척 대신 배려를" (중앙일보 2012.07.13.)

25. 김진희 "이민여성 2살 아기 집어든 복권, 100만불 '잭팟'" (중앙일보 2012.03.16.)

26. 조윤제 "사회운영 체계의 전반적 개혁 있어야" (중앙일보 2012.10.20.)

27. 어트경체첵 담딘슈렌 "한국어 호칭 너무 헷갈린다" (동아일보 인사이드 코리아 2012.03.30.)

28. *"과학기술의 발전"

29. "서열에 안주 말고 외국 대학과 경쟁할 때" (중앙일보 사설 2012.10.09.)

30. 장병희 "책 안에서 큰다, 꾸준한 독서 습관이 열쇠" (중앙일보 2012.07.15.)

31. 김혜숙 "치유로서의 인문학" (중앙일보 2012.11.15.)

32. 김창원 "'한국에 뒤지다니' 일본, 해외유학 파격 지원" (동아닷컴 2012.03.26.)

33. "대한민국 인구 5000만명 시대가 열렸다" (중앙일보 오피니언 사설 2012.06.23.)

34. 김명수 "학교 폭력 근절하려면 실상부터 알아야" (동아일보 2012.04.23.)

35. *"입시 경쟁 교육"

36. 이상언 "영어불평등 어찌할 것인가?" (중앙일보 2012.07.07.)

37. 김인택 "'학점 퍼주기'는 反교육적이다" (동아일보 2012.04.02.)

38. "운동이 최고의 명약이 되게 하려면 어떻게 해야 할까요?" (월간 가정 건강 239호, 2012.03.)

39. "스트레스 심하면 감기도 호되게 앓는다" (코메디닷컴뉴스 2012.04.04.)

40. "직업성 암 사망자 줄이는 길" (중앙일보 오피니언 사설 2012.07.03.)

41. 엄을순 "'이유 없이 여기저기 다 아프다'는 어르신 말씀, '나 우울하다'는 하소연이다"
    (중앙일보 오피니언 2012.08.06.)

42. "한국·중국계 흡연률 요지 부동: 뉴욕시 금연운동 큰 걸림돌" (한국일보 2012.03.03.)

43. "전신마비 영국 50대 '죽을 권리' 법정서 가린다" (조선닷컴 2012.03.12.)

44. "지긋지긋한 당뇨·고혈압, 알아야 이긴다" (국민건강보험 사이트)

45. 윤대현 "한국사회, 돈 잔치 결혼, 집단적 마음의 병 앓아" (조선일보 2012.03.24.)

46. 황형준 "여성 초혼 연령 29세 처음 넘어" (동아일보 2012.04.20.)

47. "아이는 이혼 부부의 소유물 아니다" (중앙일보 사설 2012.10.30.)

48. 염승은 "미국내 아시안들 "결혼은 우리끼리" 타인종간 결혼 사상 최고 불구" (중앙일보 2012.04.01.)

49. 이재웅 "더워지는 지구 힘겨운 동식물들 어떻게 살아 남을까" (동아일보 2012.01.13.)

50. 박은호 "공포의 春風" (조선일보 2012.04.04.)

* 일부 항목은 원자료의 세부사항을 확인할 수 없었음을 알려 드립니다.

지은이 **이 응 호**

- 고려대학교 영어영문학과 졸업
- 서울대학교 교육대학원 졸업
- 광희중학교, 경동고등학교 영어교사
- University of Hawaii East-West Center Diploma 취득
- Columbia University in the City of New York 응용언어학 석사 및 박사 (Fulbright 장학생)
- 수도여자사범대학 영어영문학과 교수
- 중앙대학교 영어영문학과 교수
- 미국 Defense Language Institute Foreign Language Specialist
- 한국외국어대학교 영어교육학과 교수
- 한국외국어대학교 통역대학원 교수

저서
- 『영역 한국 동화』 40권
- 『영문장 Style Guidebook』